A New Framework for Building Participation in the Arts

Kevin F. McCarthy
Kimberly Jinnett

RAND

Supported by the Wallace-Reader's Digest Funds

The research in this report was supported by the Wallace-Reader's Digest Funds.

Library of Congress Cataloging-in-Publication Data

McCarthy, Kevin F., 1945–
    A new framework for building participation in the arts / Kevin F. McCarthy.
      p. cm.
    "MR-1323."
    Includes bibliographical references.
    ISBN 0-8330-3027-2
    1. Arts—United States—Citizen participation. 2. Arts facilities—Social aspects—United
States. 3. Arts surveys—United States. I. Title.

NX230 .M37 2001
700'.973—dc21

2001034956

RAND is a nonprofit institution that helps improve policy and decisionmaking through research and analysis. RAND® is a registered trademark. RAND's publications do not necessarily reflect the opinions or policies of its research sponsors.

Cover design by Eileen Delson La Russo

Published 2001 by RAND
1700 Main Street, P.O. Box 2138, Santa Monica, CA 90407-2138
1200 South Hayes Street, Arlington, VA 22202-5050
201 North Craig Street, Suite 102, Pittsburgh, PA 15213
RAND URL: http://www.rand.org/
To order RAND documents or to obtain additional information, contact
Distribution Services: Telephone: (310) 451-7002; Fax: (310) 451-6915;
Email: order@rand.org

Arts organizations across the country are actively expanding their efforts to increase public participation in their programs. This report presents the findings of a RAND study of these efforts, the purpose of which was twofold: to better understand the process by which individuals become involved in the arts and to identify how arts institutions can most effectively influence this process. The research, sponsored by the Wallace-Reader's Digest Funds, entailed developing a behavioral model that identifies the main factors influencing individual decisions about the arts, site visits to institutions that have been particularly successful in attracting participants to their programs, and in-depth interviews with the directors of more than 100 institutions that have received grants from the Wallace-Reader's Digest Funds and the Knight Foundation to encourage greater involvement in the arts. It is hoped that this study will help arts organizations develop their own effective strategies for attracting participants.

CONTENTS

FIGURES

Many arts institutions are re-examining their missions and their roles in what has become an increasingly complex arts environment. Concurrently, arts policy appears to be shifting its focus from influencing the supply and quality of the arts to increasing the public access to and experience with the arts.

In this context, it is not surprising that many arts institutions are seeking ways to increase the public's access and exposure to their activities. They seek not only to expand their markets and increase their revenues but to broaden the definition of art and reinvigorate themselves. They face a problem, however, in determining how to go about increasing public participation. Despite their commitment, these institutions often do not have the expertise and resources needed to design and implement effective approaches. As a result, they tend to use hit-or-miss approaches, ending up uncertain about why what they tried did or did not work and thus unable to draw general lessons from their experiences.

The current research literature on arts participation offers these institutions little guidance for their participation-building efforts. This literature has two major drawbacks. First, it oversimplifies the process an individual goes through in deciding to participate in the arts, failing to take into account that the process involves more than one decision and that different factors determine the outcomes of each decision. Arts institutions thus are not provided with enough information to determine what strategies may be appropriate for encouraging the participation of those who constitute their target populations. Second, it emphasizes individuals' socio-demographics rather than their motivations and attitudes, thereby failing to provide the practical guidance institutions need if they are to influence people's participation behavior. An arts institution cannot, after all, influence an individual's background characteristics.

This report is designed to help arts institutions deal with this predicament by offering a framework that they can use to design effective strategies for building involvement in their programs. At the core of this framework is a behavioral model of the decisionmaking process. In addition, the framework provides an integrative approach for organizations to use when implementing the model, and a set of practical guidelines to apply to this process. Our model is predicated on the assumption that to influence behavior, one must understand how the decisionmaking process actually works. Indeed, a behavioral model must not simply identify factors correlated with a certain behavior, it must specify how those factors operate. Our model attempts to capture the complexity of the decisionmaking process by recognizing that an individual's decision to participate in the arts is really a set of decisions and involves a complex mix of attitudes, intentions, constraints, and behaviors, as well as feedback between that mix and past experience.

Key to our model is the idea that the participation decision is a process divisible into separate stages, each affected by different factors. The *background stage* consists of the individual's general attitudes toward the arts; *stage 1* is the individual's formation of a predisposition to participate in the arts; *stage 2* is his or her evaluation of specific participation opportunities; and *stage 3* is the individual's actual participation experience and subsequent assessment of his or her inclination to participate. Each of these stages is influenced by a different set of factors. What influences the background stage are the individual's *background* characteristics--socio-demographics, personality traits, prior arts experience, and socio-cultural factors. Stage 1 is influenced by *perceptual* factors, such as personal beliefs about the benefits and costs of arts participation and perceptions of how reference groups view the arts; Stage 2 by *practical* factors, such as available information on the arts, the costs involved in participation, and convenience; and stage 3 by the individual's reaction to the actual *experience*.

The model recognizes that the critical issue in designing and implementing effective participation strategies is knowing what the appropriate tactics are and when to use them. The guidance it provides on this issue underscores how important it is for an institution to align its participation goal (to diversify participation—i.e., attract new markets; to broaden participation—i.e., attract new members from existing markets; or to deepen participation—i.e., increase the level of involvement of participants) with its target population (those not disposed to participate, those disposed to participate but not currently doing so, or those already participating) and to focus its tactics on the behavioral levers appropriate for that population. It also provides specific examples of potential tactics.

The model also recognizes that information is critical to the engagement process and must flow back and forth between potential participants and arts organizations. For example, if arts institutions are to design effective engagement strategies, they must know where their target populations are in the decision-making process with regard to arts participation, what motivates their participation, and specifics about their lifestyles and programmatic interests.

Similarly, if potential participants are to make informed choices, they need information about arts organizations and what they have to offer. What information they need will depend on where they are in the decisionmaking process. Those not disposed to participate will need information about the benefits the arts can provide them (i.e., information to convince them that the arts are worth their participation), whereas those disposed to participate but not currently doing so will need information telling them what activities are offered, when and where, and at what price. Those already involved with the arts will benefit from information that increases their understanding and knowledge of the arts.

Our approach recognizes that in designing and implementing their engagement strategies, arts institutions must also be mindful of their resource constraints and other institutional goals. Indeed, failure to consider their broader institutional and community contexts can create conflicts within the organization and make setting priorities and goals very difficult. Thus, our framework suggests that institutions must determine how participation building efforts fit with their overall purpose and mission, their available resources, and the community environment in which they operate. In other words, arts organizations must take an integrative approach to building participation, one that

- Links the organization's participation-building activities to its core values and purpose through goals chosen to support that purpose.

- Identifies clear target groups and bases its tactics on good information about those groups.

- Clearly understands both the internal and external resources that can be committed to building participation.

- Establishes a process for feedback and self-evaluation.

Although we believe that arts organizations should tailor the strategies and tactics they use to build participation to their specific target populations and institutional contexts, our framework offers a set of guidelines to help institutions approach the task of participation building. These guidelines provide suggestions as to how institutions should approach the process as a whole as well as each of its central elements.

ACKNOWLEDGMENTS

We want to thank the various individuals whose assistance was instrumental in this research. First, we would like to express our appreciation to the staff at the Wallace-Reader's Digest Funds, especially Ed Pauly and Michael Moore and former staff member Holly Sidford, for their encouragement, advice, and assistance throughout the course of our work. We would also like to thank the individuals and institutions we contacted during our site visits and surveys for their willingness to share their experiences and insights with us.

We also acknowledge the helpful comments and suggestions of Sue Bodilly and Jerry Yoshitomi, who reviewed an earlier draft of this report. We are indebted to fellow project members Tessa Kaganoff, Brent Keltner, Elizabeth Ondaatje, and Ann Stone for their assistance and suggestions. Finally, we owe a special thanks to Laura Zakaras, who read and commented on various drafts, and to Lisa Lewis for all her help in the conduct of the research and the production of this report.

Chapter One

INTRODUCTION

Over the past decade, many arts institutions have been devoting more attention and resources to increasing public participation in their activities. Typically, however, they find themselves in something of a predicament. Their limited resources and staffs make it imperative that they employ participation-building strategies that will be effective, and yet they typically find inadequate guidance, particularly from the existing research literature, on how to proceed. As a result, they often end up using hit-or-miss approaches, which leave them uncertain about why what they tried did or did not work and thus unable to draw general lessons from their experiences. This report is designed specifically to provide information that will help arts institutions deal with this predicament. What we offer is a framework for designing and implementing strategies for influencing people's participation in the arts. This framework consists of a behavioral model for understanding how people decide to participate, an integrative approach for organizations to use when implementing the model, and a set of guidelines to apply to this task.

BACKGROUND

Cultural institutions are seeking ways to adapt to what is a changing arts world in the United States. The organizational demography of the arts world is being restructured: small nonprofit and community-based arts organizations are proliferating; large nonprofit and commercial arts institutions pursue strategies enabling them to adjust to technological developments that are changing what art is produced and how art is distributed. Furthermore, although the gap between earned revenues and costs that was identified over three decades ago (Baumol and Bowen, 1966) still requires nonprofit arts institutions to patch together financial support from a diverse mix of public and private sources, raising funds has in many ways become more of a challenge. Corporations increasingly target their support (Useem, 1990; Cobb, 1996); foundations now look for evidence that their grants produce broader benefits (Renz and Lawrence, 1998); and government support has increasingly shifted from the federal to the state and local levels (DiMaggio, 1991), in the process becoming focused less on the arts per se and more on the social and economic benefits arts bring to local communities.

An increase in the supply of arts—particularly the dramatic increase in small nonprofit arts institutions—has sparked a corresponding increase in arts participation (National Endowment for the Arts, 1997). This increase appears, however, to be more connected with amateur "hands-on" arts activities and arts participation through the media than with attendance at live performances. In fact, attendance at live arts performances seems to have remained relatively stable over the past two decades—both in terms of the fraction of the population who attend (attendance rates) (National Endowment for the Arts, 1997) and in terms of their socio-economic selectivity (Robinson, 1993).

To adapt to these changes in the arts environment, arts institutions have begun to re-examine their missions and their roles. Moreover, they are facing these challenges at a time when what used to be seen as separate and distinct commercial, nonprofit, and community-based volunteer sectors are increasingly viewed as different elements of a single, diversified arts environment (Cherbo and Wyszomirski, 2000).

At the same time, the public debate about arts policy has shifted, moving from what sometimes appeared to be an exclusive focus on public funding for the nonprofit sector to a more general concern with the public benefits of the arts and how each sector of the art world promotes those benefits (American Assembly, 2000). In calling on arts organizations to more explicitly consider and support the public benefits of the arts, the American Assembly acknowledged that the arts community has tended to view arts policy solely in terms of its impact on artists and arts organizations. It also identified broad categories of public benefits at the individual, community, and national levels.

The arts serve as a source of entertainment, enrichment, and fulfillment at the individual level. In addition, they can promote openness to new ideas and creativity as well as competencies at school and work. At the community level, the arts can provide a variety of social and economic benefits, such as increasing the level of economic activity, creating a more livable environment, and promoting a sense of community pride. At the national level, the arts express the country's rich cultural diversity and pluralism, reinforce national identity, and provide an important body of cultural goods for international export.

The focus of most arts policy has traditionally been on the "supply side" (Chapman, 1992)—that is, on influencing the quality and quantity of arts available by supporting arts organizations—but the new emphasis on the public benefits of the arts requires that the focus be on the "demand side"—that is, on increasing the public's access and exposure to the arts. Thus, for example, the role of the arts as a source of individual entertainment and enrichment and the various instrumental benefits the arts can provide at the individual, community, and national level are predicated on increasing the number and diversity of people who participate as well as the depth of their participation.

In this context, it is not surprising that many arts institutions have looked to provide greater service to their communities and to reach out to local populations that traditionally have not participated in their activities. Their goal is not just to expand their market and increase their revenues, but also to broaden their definition of art and reinvigorate themselves.

THE PREDICAMENT

In setting out to increase public participation in their activities, arts institutions face a series of strategic and tactical choices for which they are often unprepared. At the strategic level, they must decide what their goals are and why. At the tactical level, they must decide how to accomplish their goals. Moreover, most nonprofit arts institutions face severe resource constraints,[1] so the strategic and tactical choices they make about goals and approaches will affect not only the success of their participation-building efforts, but also the resources available for programming and other artistic and organizational activities.

A central strategic issue involves deciding what an institution means when it says it wants to increase participation. An institution can increase participation in three basic ways: (1) by *broadening* it—i.e., capturing a larger share of the existing market by attracting individuals who constitute a natural audience for the arts but are not currently participants; (2) by *deepening* it—i.e., intensifying its current participants' level of involvement; and (3) by *diversifying* it—i.e., attracting new markets comprising those individuals who typically would not entertain the idea of participating in the arts. An institution could decide to pursue all three of these paths, but we believe (and will demonstrate later) that doing so poses a difficult challenge, because each of these markets requires a different engagement strategy. Indeed, if what constitutes an appropriate strategy depends on which group an arts organization decides to target, choosing a target population constitutes a central component of the goal-setting process.

---

[1]We surveyed 102 arts organizations during the course of our research. When asked to name the single greatest challenge to their participation-building efforts, these organizations consistently cited the difficulty of balancing competing demands against their available resources. When asked to name the three biggest challenges his organization faced, one respondent said, "First, dollars; second, dollars; and third, dollars."

The central tactical issues revolve around (1) identifying the behavioral levers appropriate for influencing participation and (2) matching the resources needed to manipulate these levers to the resources the institution has available internally and from the community. In choosing their tactics, institutions need to consider not just what to do but when and for whom. Lowering prices, for example, may be enough to convince some potential participants to "give it a try" but may have little or no effect on other populations. As noted above, the obstacles associated with convincing people to increase their participation appear to vary depending on whether those people are inclined to participate but not yet doing so, already participating, or disinclined to participate.

Clearly, then, arts institutions hoping to increase participation in their activities face complex issues that require a systematic understanding of arts participation behavior. Since arts organization staff typically have artistic or arts management rather than research or marketing backgrounds, they most likely will not have the information they need to address these issues. Many arts institutions, including the ones we interviewed during the course of this study, have hired marketing personnel to help them design and implement their participation-building activities. However, knowing how to market the arts is not really equivalent to understanding the dynamics of the process individuals go through in deciding whether to participate in the arts.

Usually in a situation like this, the research literature would be of help. But by and large, the research literature on arts participation does not provide the needed answers (McCarthy and Zakaras, forthcoming). Instead, it is much more likely to address the who, what, and how of arts participation rather than why people behave as they do. Most research studies on this topic describe who participates, how often, and in what ways. And the studies that do examine participants' motivations focus on the explicit reasons individuals cite for their decisions rather than how they reached their decisions. This distinction is important, because if one wants to influence people's decisions, one must understand the dynamics of the decisionmaking process. In other words, it is not enough to simply identify the factors that are correlated with the behavior. One must also specify how their effects are transmitted and how and where intervention in the decisionmaking process can influence the outcome.

METHODOLOGY

We gathered our information for the analysis in several ways—by exploring the literature on the subject, by conducting site visits at 13 arts institutions, and by conducting a telephone survey of 102 arts organizations in the United States. The first of these, the literature review, is reported on in Chapter Two.

The site visits were designed to provide us with a qualitative understanding of how individual arts organizations approach the task of building participation. We discussed a wide range of topics during each of these visits: how the organization defined its participation goals; how those goals related to its broader mission; how it designed and implemented its participation strategies; what tactics it used; how it interacted with its broader communities, target populations, and artists; how it defined and measured progress toward its goals; and what it viewed as major challenges to its participation-building programs. The 13 institutions were selected from a list of organizations that received support from the Wallace-Reader's Digest Funds (referred to throughout this document as *the Funds*) and whose participation-building activities the Funds regarded as exemplary. These institutions represented different artistic disciplines and locations, had different resource levels, and were serving different target populations. Many of the conclusions discussed in Chapter Five are based on what we learned during these site visits.

The 102 arts organizations that we surveyed either had received or were receiving support from the Funds and the Knight Foundation. Our survey was designed to collect quantitative and systematic information about the characteristics of these organizations and the specific things they did to increase participation. The sample we used was chosen after stratifying the Funds' current and former grantees based on organizational mission, artistic discipline, and location—information supplied by the Funds. The initial sample consisted of 108 institutions, 102 of which completed the survey.

As we discuss in more detail in Appendix A, the sample we used is not representative of arts organizations as a whole. Both the Funds and the Knight Foundation have been particularly interested in building public participation in the arts, so it is reasonable to expect that their grantees would be more focused on increasing participation than would arts organizations chosen at random. Moreover, these institutions often were selected for the grants because of their specific characteristics (the Funds' grants to visual arts organizations, for example, purposely focused on those with large budgets) or because they promised to employ specific tactics in their participation-building activities. In sum, the data we used provide a rich source of systematic information on these organizations and their participation-building activities, but they do not allow for a generalization to arts institutions as a whole. Appendix A covers the characteristics of the organizations surveyed; Appendix B covers the organizations' participation-building activities.

A NOTE ON TERMINOLOGY

Most of the literature on participation uses the term *audience development* to describe the efforts of arts organizations to increase the populations they serve.

More recently, there has been a shift to the term *building participation* because it avoids the connotation that people experience the arts exclusively by attending live performances or visiting a museum. The arts are an interactive experience, and participation can be enhanced in a number of ways other than merely increasing audience size. In this report, we use both terms to mean enhancing arts participation in the broadest sense.

In discussing what organizations do to increase participation, we refer to specific items—such as how they publicize their activities or gain information on potential participants—as *tactics*. We refer to their general overall approach, or set of tactics, as their *strategy*. Thus, *strategy* is the more general term, and tactics are subsumed within strategies.

Finally, we use *engagement activities* and *participation-building activities* interchangeably to describe the processes by which arts institutions seek to interact with people to spur them to participate.

ORGANIZATION OF THE REPORT

Chapter Two discusses the research literature on arts participation, summarizes the key findings, and highlights several important features of the decisionmaking process. Chapter Three presents our behavioral model, describing how it incorporates and explains important features of an individual's decisionmaking process. Chapter Four sets out guidelines for developing effective strategies and tactics in conjunction with the model; Chapter Five discusses why effective participation building requires an integrative approach; and Chapter Six restates our conclusions from the earlier chapters and summarizes all of the framework's guidelines. Appendices A and B detail the survey results. Appendix C provides details on the site visits.

Chapter Two

THE PARTICIPATION LITERATURE

The literature on participation generally falls into two categories: empirical studies describing patterns of participation behavior, and theoretical studies seeking to explain that behavior. Both types of studies provide important insights into participation behavior; neither, however, directly addresses the issues facing arts institutions as they attempt to design and implement effective participation-building strategies. This chapter summarizes the key features of the research literature, highlights the key findings, and discusses why the literature fails to provide the needed information.

Before we begin with these topics, however, two definitional issues must be resolved: How do we define participation in the arts? And what activities do we include in our definition of the arts?

Although participation in the arts is sometimes discussed as though it were a homogeneous phenomenon, it can take several forms. Individuals may participate in a "hands-on" way—e.g., by singing in a choir or painting a picture. They may also participate through attendance—e.g., by going to a ballet or visiting an art museum. And they may participate through the media—e.g., by listening to an opera on the radio, playing a jazz CD, or watching a play on television. Separating the three ways of participating is important. Consider, for instance, that according to the empirical literature, more people participate in the arts through the media than through attendance, and many more participate through attendance than through hands-on engagement (National Endowment for the Arts, 1998; Americans for the Arts, 1996). As we document in Chapter Five, arts institutions' missions and ways of interacting with participants often differ. All institutions are interested in increasing attendance, and many are likely to be interested in providing opportunities to involve people with the arts in a hands-on way,[1] but participation in the arts through the media is less

---

[1]Several of the institutions we interviewed placed a very high priority on getting participants directly involved in the arts creation process.

directly relevant to their participation-building activities. In other words, these three forms of participation are not equally relevant to arts institutions trying to increase public involvement in their activities.

As for how we define the arts, that, of course, is considerably more problematic than defining participation in that it involves aesthetic and philosophical questions well beyond the scope of our research. It is important to note, however, that which activities are included in this definition directly affects estimates of participation levels (Walker et al., 2000; AMS, 1995; Robinson, 1993) and may affect the individual's decisionmaking process as well. There is no consensus on which types of art activities should be included. There is general agreement about the so-called classic arts—opera, ballet, dance, theater, classical music, painting and sculpture, and literature—but the same cannot be said for the more popular art forms, such as rock and roll, hip-hop, and activities provided by the commercial entertainment industries (film, radio, and television). There is also no consensus on whether to include amateur arts and crafts. The estimates of participation levels cited in this report are based on the definitions of the National Endowment for the Arts (NEA) Survey of Public Participation in the Arts (SPPA).

EMPIRICAL LITERATURE

Much of the empirical literature is based on analyses of individual survey data—in particular, NEA's SPPA (National Endowment for the Arts, 1997).[2] This literature principally focuses on three aspects of participation behavior: levels of participation, characteristics of participants, and the reasons people cite for their participation.

Levels of Participation

The arts are a popular leisure time activity for a large proportion of the population. According to the most recent survey data (National Endowment for the Arts, 1998), about 50 percent of all adults in the United States attended a performance in one of seven performing arts (jazz, classical music, opera, musicals, nonmusical plays, ballet, and other dance) or visited an art museum in the preceding year.[3] Although the attendance rates for this form of participation are

---

[2]The Harris poll surveys conducted for Americans for the Arts (Americans for the Arts, 1996) provide a second major source of survey data on arts participation at the individual level. The SPPA data are used more frequently because, compared to the Harris poll survey data, they contain a broader range of information about individuals and their participation.

[3]The participation data cited here are reported in NEA's report on the latest SPPA (National Endowment for the Arts, 1998).

below those for more popular forms of entertainment—such as watching television (which is virtually universal) and attending films—they nonetheless compare favorably with those for such other leisure time activities as attending sports events or going to an amusement park.

The survey data also show that over three-quarters of the adult U.S. population watched or listened to an arts performance or a program about the arts through the media, and about two-thirds participated directly through hands-on experiences—for example, by playing an instrument, painting or sculpting, writing, or taking photographs. These latter activities are comparable in popularity to such non-arts activities as gardening, exercising, and camping.

Although the literature does not specifically address why some forms of participation are more popular than others, it appears that the answer may be related in part to ready availability. Watching television (which consumes about three hours of every American's day, according to Robinson and Godbey, 1997) and listening to the radio or a CD are ideally suited to filling small bits of time, can be done simultaneously with other activities, and are possible at almost any time for most people. Thus, participation through the media is flexible in that it can be fit into most people's schedules more or less by choice. Hands-on activities are also flexible, but attending live performances, which are usually scheduled for specific times and places, is much less so.

Rates of participation vary not only with the form of participation but also with the type of art. Whether participation is through attendance, the media, or hands-on engagement, rates of participation are lowest for opera and ballet, intermediate for classical music and jazz, and highest for theater and musicals. Very little is known about why arts participants choose one type of art over another. The literature on individual motivations indicates that interest in the programmed material is a relatively important factor in the decision to attend a specific performance (Ford Foundation, 1974), but this fact does not explain why an individual chooses one type of art rather than another. How relevant the programmed material is to the individual is also likely to play a role, but this connection has not been researched. And as discussed above, an individual's ability to tailor participation to his or her own schedule and tastes—i.e., the flexibility of form of participation—may also play a role.[4]

In comparing participation levels, the issue of crossover effects also arises. Crossover effects in arts participation could come about in one of two ways: (1) a person who takes part in the arts through one form of participation may be

_____

[4]It is interesting to note that art museums, which have higher attendance rates than do any of the performing arts, have greater flexibility in terms of the hours they are open and the material they offer.

more inclined to take part through another form—e.g., if he participates through the media (say, watches arts programs on television), he may be more apt to attend live arts performances; and (2) a person who participates in a particular type of art may be more inclined to participate in another—e.g., if she attends live symphony performances, she may be more likely to attend musicals. Love, in a major study of crossover effects in the arts (Love, 1995), suggests that crossover effects are more the exception than the rule. He found that with a few notable exceptions—e.g., jazz lovers are very likely to attend performances, listen to recordings, and watch programs about jazz, and people who watch television programs about one type of art are very likely to watch programs about other types—crossover effects are not typical of arts participation.[5]

In attempting to compare participation rates over time, we encountered complications due to changes in survey procedures and much higher refusal rates in the most recent (1997) SPPA data. The data available indicate that total attendance at live performances increased between 4 and 16 percent from 1982 to 1997. Most of this increase, however, appears to be a product of population growth and increasing educational levels within the population. In contrast, the rates of participation through the media and through hands-on engagement appear to have increased.

Who Participates

Virtually all studies of arts participation include some analysis of the individual characteristics associated with being a participant. Of these, education is by far the most closely correlated with all three forms of participation in the arts (National Endowment for the Arts, 1998; Robinson, 1993; Schuster, 1991).[6] Individuals with higher levels of education—particularly those with college and graduate degrees—have much higher participation rates than individuals with less education. However, this connection appears to be stronger for those who participate through attendance rather than through the media and is least pronounced for hands-on participants (National Endowment for the Arts, 1998).

What drives this education effect is not altogether clear. More highly educated individuals are more likely to have been exposed to the arts during the course of

---

[5]It should be noted that these comparisons were made using the population in general. It is quite possible that a comparison's structure may well affect its results. Thus, for instance, the degree of crossover found may well depend on whether one uses as the standard the percentage of participants in the less frequent activity (e.g., hands-on participation) who also attend live performances or the percentage of participants in the more frequent activity (e.g., participation through the media) who also attend live performances or participate through hands-on engagement. Unfortunately, there is no empirical evidence on such differences.

[6]The effects of education are also observed across disciplines. See, for example, National Endowment for the Arts, 1998; Deveaux, 1994; Holak et al., 1986; Keagen, 1987; Lemmons, 1966.

their education—and familiarity with and knowledge of the arts are directly re-lated to arts participation, as is the case for most types of leisure activities, i.e., the more familiarity and knowledge, the more participation (Kelley and Freisinger, 2000). Education also helps individuals develop skill in dealing with the abstract—a skill useful for appreciating the arts (Toffler, 1964). The fact (noted above) that the effects of education appear to be most pronounced in comparisons of attendance, which is the most social form of participation, sug-gests that social factors—e.g., prestige, the influence of friends and relatives, and what those friends and relatives view as preferred forms of entertainment—are also important.

The findings for other socio-demographic factors are more ambiguous. While gender and age matter, they are less important than education. Age appears to have a more pronounced effect on hands-on participation rates than on the other participation rates (Peters and Cherbo, 1996), and rates of attendance and through-the-media participation do not vary significantly with age (after con-trolling for other factors) except after age 65. Such other factors as marital status, political ideology, income, and race all appear to be associated with dif-ferences in participation rates at first glance, but their efforts tend to disappear once education is controlled for.

Along with these variables, the literature also examines the relationship be-tween participation and background factors such as arts education and contact with the arts as a child (Bergonzi and Smith, 1996; Orend and Keegan, 1996). Both of these factors have been shown to be strongly associated with increased participation. Moreover, these effects appear to hold even after education levels are controlled for. Orend and Keegan (1996) suggest that the effects of arts so-cialization (in the form of arts education classes and more contacts with the arts) are particularly important for explaining differences in participation rates among the less-well-educated.

Finally, studies of the frequency with which the population participates in the arts indicate that the distribution of participation is highly skewed: a relatively small percentage of the population accounts for the vast majority of total arts participation.[7] People can generally be sorted into three categories based on their arts participation: those who rarely (if ever) participate, those who partici-pate infrequently, and those who participate frequently.

---

[7]The most comprehensive analysis of this phenomenon is one done by Schuster (1991) for art museum attendance. However, it has also been noted by Robinson et al. (1985) and Robinson (1993) for the performing arts.

Motivations for Participation

To understand individuals' motivations for participation, three questions must be addressed: Why do people participate in the arts rather than in other leisure activities? Why do they participate in different ways—through attendance, through the media, and through hands-on engagement? And why do they choose specific types of art? Each of these questions addresses a different aspect of participation. The first relates to overall levels of demand; the other two refer to the ways that demand is distributed by form of participation and type of art. The empirical literature addresses the first question but rarely addresses the other two.

By and large, studies of participants' motivations focus on the reasons individuals give for deciding whether to attend or not attend performances (Ford Foundation, 1974; National Endowment for the Arts, 1998; Robinson, 1993). These studies highlight a variety of practical and contextual factors—e.g., costs, availability, information, scheduling—that drive individual decisions. Interestingly, the importance attached to these factors appears to depend on whether the individual is a rare, occasional, or frequent participant in the arts. Those who frequently attend but would like to attend more are most likely to cite practical factors as an important consideration. For those who attend occasionally or rarely, these factors are less important (Schuster, 1991). This finding suggests that the participation behavior of frequent, occasional, and rare participants may be motivated by different factors.

In addition to studies of individual decisions, the empirical literature includes studies seeking to explain shifts that drive demand for the arts at the aggregate level (Urice, 1992; Butsch, 2000). Four sets of factors in particular have been used to explain changes in overall demand: changes in the population's size and composition; changes in people's taste for the arts; changes in practical factors (such as availability, income, prices, and time) that affect individuals' ability to realize their preferences for the arts; and changes in the stock of knowledge about the arts. These factors affect participation in expected ways. For example, arts participation has been shown to increase as the population grows, as education levels increase, as the arts become more available or less expensive relative to other leisure activities, and as more people are exposed to the arts as children or in school. Understanding the dynamic behind changes in tastes is less straightforward because it relates to a question not typically addressed in the empirical literature: What are the underlying determinants of individual tastes?

Indeed, because the empirical work on participation is constrained by the data available and by the limits of those data, comprehensive explanations for participation behavior are much more likely to be found in the theoretical literature.

THEORETICAL LITERATURE

Compared to the empirical literature on arts participation, the theoretical literature is much less extensive. The social sciences in general have not been particularly successful in constructing theories that systematically explain participation behavior. The most comprehensive work can be found in the economics literature, which approaches participation decisions within the framework of a general model of consumer behavior (Heilbrun and Gray, 1993). Most of the theoretical work within the other social science disciplines can be viewed as complementing the economics approach by focusing on the determinants of individual tastes. The research literature on leisure, while not offering a comprehensive framework for explaining arts behavior, does offer several important insights into that behavior.

Economic Approaches

In the traditional economic approach to participation behavior, individuals are assumed to be rational consumers who seek to maximize satisfaction (utility) by choosing a level of arts participation that satisfies their preferences for the arts, subject to constraints of income and price. An individual's preferences, or tastes, are assumed to be fixed and to depend on a host of individual characteristics (socio-demographic and psychological factors) largely assumed to be "outside" the model.

Income and price play the key roles in this framework. In general, as the price of participation increases, individuals participate less. *Price* here refers to the price of arts participation and related activities (e.g., admission costs, transportation, childcare) and the price of alternative goods or leisure activities that are "substitutes" for arts participation. Thus, the level of arts participation depends on the price of participation relative to the price of substitute leisure activities (Throsby and Winter, 1979; Vogel, 2000; Nardone, 1982).

Conversely, as income rises, participation should rise. However, the direct effects of rising income may be partly offset by the "opportunity costs" of participation—i.e., the earnings forgone by spending one's time participating in the arts rather than working. The tradeoff between the direct (and positive) earnings effect and the indirect (and negative) opportunity-cost effect varies with an individual's preference for the arts relative to other goods and leisure activities and with his or her income level. The greater an individual's taste for the arts, the more likely the income effect will dominate. In addition, the opportunity-cost effect appears to dominate at lower and moderate income levels, whereas the income effect dominates at higher income levels—a pattern that helps explain higher participation levels among higher-income (and thus among better-educated) individuals (Felton, 1992).

Stigler and Becker (1977) offer a reformulation of the traditional economic model. They suggest that the satisfaction and enjoyment individuals derive from the arts depend not simply on income, price, and tastes but also on such factors as prior artistic experience, knowledge of the arts, education, and family background (which are normally viewed as correlates of taste) because these factors allow individuals to become more effective consumers of the arts. In other words, the more experience and familiarity an individual has with the arts, the more enjoyment he or she is able to derive from a particular level of consumption.

The economics literature offers two important insights into the arts participation decision. First, it highlights the role that practical factors such as price, income, information, and leisure alternatives play in individuals' participation decisions. For example, as the price of arts participation increases (either directly, in the form of higher admissions and related costs, or indirectly, in the form of its relationship to the price of other leisure activities), participation will decline. Also, as consumers gain more information on the availability and prices of arts activities relative to those of other leisure activities, participation rates will change, the direction of the change depending on the outcome of the comparison. And as the range of substitute leisure activities expands, arts participation will be affected by the individual's having more alternatives to choose from.

The second insight from the economics literature is the idea that the more knowledgeable people are about the arts, the more likely they are to participate, because they gain more satisfaction and enjoyment from a given level of consumption than do people who are less knowledgeable. This effect provides a potential explanation for why participation levels vary as sharply as they do among rare, occasional, and frequent arts consumers. It also helps to explain why some people use the term *addiction* for the love that art aficionados (those who are enthusiastic fans of the arts) have for the arts.

Other Conceptual Approaches

As indicated above, noneconomic studies of arts participation are apt to pursue a descriptive rather than a conceptual approach. However, these studies can be viewed as complementing the economic approach by focusing on the empirical correlates of participation as proxies for individual tastes. Thus, the work of sociologists who focus on such socio-demographic correlates of participation as education, family background, gender, and ethnicity can be viewed as identifying the background characteristics that determine individuals' tastes. Similarly, psychologists, who focus on personality and related individual characteristics, can be viewed as elucidating the psychological factors that may predispose individuals to participate in the arts.[8]

Perhaps the most useful body of conceptual literature on participation is the interdisciplinary work on leisure activity (Kelley, 1987). Although this literature does not offer a fully integrated theory of participation, it provides several important concepts for understanding individuals' arts participation decisions. These concepts are particularly useful for addressing those motivational issues that, as we noted above, have not been adequately dealt with in the empirical literature: relative preferences for the arts versus other leisure activities, for particular types of art, and for particular forms of participation.

For example, the leisure literature identifies the amount and nature of the leisure time available to an individual as being central to his or her leisure choices. Underlying this point is the recognition that an individual's time can be used in one of three ways (Robinson and Godbey, 1997): for work and work-related activities (e.g., commuting), for the basic necessities of life (e.g., sleeping, eating, dressing), and for discretionary, or leisure, activities. Since the amount of time in a day is fixed, more time spent in any one of these ways means less available time for the other two. Moreover, because the amount of time an individual spends tending to life's basic necessities is relatively fixed, the major tradeoff tends to be between work and leisure.

How an individual chooses to spend his or her leisure time will be directly influenced by the amount of that time and how it is structured. As the amount of leisure time decreases, the opportunity costs of that time will increase and the individual will thus become more selective. As an individual's leisure time becomes increasingly fragmented—whether due to irregular work schedules, family responsibilities, or something else—he or she is likely to become increasingly selective about how to use any "free" time. Leisure activities that do not fit into the busy schedule will lose out, while those that are most adaptable to it will become more popular. Robinson and Godbey (1997) refer to this phenomenon as "leisure by appointment" and suggest that it has become increasingly common.

---

[8]A particularly interesting example of this approach is the work of Zaltman (1998), who has identified a basic set of constructs, metaphors, and themes that individuals use to describe their experiences with the arts. As Zaltman suggests, these themes provide considerable insight into the way the arts resonate with people on a deep psychological level.

A major reason for this pattern may well be the changing availability and in-creasing fragmentation of leisure time in U.S. society. Although the growth in leisure time enjoyed in the United States for much of the 20th century has re-versed for some segments of the population, it is unclear whether it has for Americans in general. Robinson and Godbey (1997) argue that with a few no-table exceptions, Americans now have as much available leisure time as they did in the past. Schor (1991) argues the reverse. Most observers do agree, how-ever, that the structure of leisure time has become more fragmented as a result of increasingly irregular work schedules in the United States (Vogel, 2000), and that this phenomenon is especially true for the more highly educated, who are the heaviest consumers of the arts.

According to Putnam (2000), the perception of reduced leisure time and a growing focus on home-centered leisure activities have increased the competi-tion that the arts, especially the live performing arts, face from other leisure activities. Although the emphasis in the leisure literature is on how leisure time constraints affect the choice between participating in the arts versus other leisure activities, these constraints also affect choices among types of art. As we suggested earlier, a reason for the observed differences in attendance rates may be the flexibility offered by specific activities. An individual visiting an art mu-seum can choose when to visit, how much time to spend, and what to view and not to view. An individual does not have this same flexibility when attending a live event, which usually takes place at a specific time, lasts for a specific dura-tion, and presents a set program.

A second contribution of the leisure literature is the insight it offers into the motivations of arts aficionados—those people who are devoted followers of the arts. Unlike the economics literature, which explains the arts aficionado phe-nomenon in terms of the increasing satisfaction that familiarity with the arts brings, the leisure literature tends to view it more in psychological terms: a small fraction of the participants in leisure activities become serious "amateurs" for whom the activity becomes an end in itself (Stebbins, 1992). As Kelley and Freisinger (2000) point out, this phenomenon is common to a wide range of leisure activities in which there is a progression in commitment to the activity. As their commitment grows, the individuals come to define themselves in terms of the activity, or in their words, "It becomes central to who one is" (pp. 82–83). Indeed, the individual sometimes becomes part of a community of individuals and almost all of his or her friends share this same activity. This type of community of interest has also been identified by Putnam (2000) as a major need in current U.S. society.

A final important insight that the leisure literature offers concerns the factors that influence an individual's decision about how to participate—i.e., through attendance, the media, or hands-on engagement. In this case, one suggestion from the literature is that a useful framework for analyzing this decision is to consider two different dimensions of a person's choices: Is this person primarily seeking entertainment or fulfillment? Does he or she prefer to participate alone or with others? (Kelley and Freisinger, 2000; Kelley, 1987). The first of these dimensions distinguishes between activities primarily undertaken as a form of entertainment, such as watching television (Robinson and Godbey, 1997), and those undertaken for enrichment or self-fulfillment, or what has been referred to as "serious leisure" (Stebbins, 1992). The second dimension pertains to the social context: Is the social experience equally as or more important than the activity itself, or is the individual's main motivation self-focused—i.e., is he or she primarily interested in developing proficiency in the activity?

Combined, these two dimensions provide a framework for distinguishing among different types of arts participants (see Figure 2.1). Within the group of individuals primarily seeking entertainment, those who are self-focused will be more inclined to participate through the media (by, for example, listening to recorded music or watching a play on television), and those seeking a social experience, the "casual attendees," will be more inclined to attend a live performance. Within the group primarily desiring enrichment and self-fulfillment, the self-focused will be inclined to engage in hands-on activities, and those seeking the social experience will be "aficionado attendees."

People falling into a particular cell of this classification scheme are not precluded from participating in other ways. Those who primarily participate in the arts through the media may also attend live performances, as may hands-on participants. Moreover, regardless of their form of participation, individuals will also choose from the various art forms, both the high and the more popular. However, this basic scheme provides a useful device for recognizing that individuals' motivations for participation and the predominant form that participation is likely to take will differ and that these differences are important to bear in mind when developing an outreach strategy.

		What Person Seeks	
		Entertainment	Fulfillment
Participation Preference	Developing proficiency (self-focused)	Participation through media	Hands-on participation
	Social experience	Attendance (casual)	Attendance (aficionado)

Figure 2.1—Framework Explaining Forms of Participation

These differences may be particularly useful for arts institutions seeking to increase attendance at live performances. For example, the scheme suggests that the market for live performing arts consists of two distinct groups: casual attendees and aficionados. Casual attendees differ from aficionados not only in their motivations but also in their numbers, knowledge of the arts, and in all probability their tastes. The aficionados are the frequent attendees discussed above. They are a small and select group of people likely to be knowledgeable about and interested in a diverse array of content. The casual attendees, in contrast, are likely to be far more numerous, less interested in the art form per se, and more likely to be attracted to programming that is more traditional or that relates directly to their daily lives.

These findings suggest several points for arts institutions to consider when developing strategies to increase participation. First, they need to be mindful of how their activities fit into the schedules of their target populations. Second, they need to be aware that potential participants have many leisure activity options (both art and non-art) open to them and thus need to know how what is being offered compares with those other options. Third, given potential participants' limited leisure time and increasing entertainment options, arts institutions must consider the nature of the target groups, their motivations, and how the institution's programming relates to those motivations. The insights suggest that very different engagement strategies may be needed to increase participation among the three groups: those who rarely (if ever) participate in the arts, those who participate occasionally, and those who participate frequently. Finally, arts institutions must realize that the process of converting individuals from rare to occasional to frequent participants is likely to require a significant transformation in those individuals' commitment to the arts and that this process is likely to be long (Morrison and Dalgleish, 1987). However, once the transformation occurs, those individuals may well become part of the institution's community and, as such, will be not only habitual attendees but also volunteers, contributors, and board members.

CRITIQUE OF PARTICIPATION LITERATURE

Despite providing a variety of information about participation behavior and its dynamics, the participation literature is unlikely to provide adequate guidance for arts institutions interested in building participation for two reasons. First, it leaves many important questions about participation behavior unanswered; second, and more important, it fails to capture the complexity of the decision-making process. In fact, the complexity of the participation behavior documented in the empirical literature is not even reflected in the conceptual approaches offered in the theoretical literature.

Unanswered Questions

Given limited data and the tendency of that data to focus more on description than on explanation, the literature's having largely ignored several issues about participation is probably not surprising. As noted above, very little is known about why individuals prefer one type of art activity to another or why they choose one form of arts participation over another. Nor does anyone really understand much about the reasons individuals cite for their participation decisions. How does one explain, for example, the diversity of those reasons?

Moreover, it is not known how certain factors that have been demonstrated to be correlated with participation behavior actually operate. For example, education has been found to be strongly associated with arts participation, but why this is so is unclear. We cannot explain, for example, why even though most regular arts participants are highly educated, not all well-educated individuals are arts participants, or why many less-well-educated individuals are regular arts participants. The same general point can be made about any of the factors that are correlated with participation, most notably arts education and exposure to the arts as a child. Although these various socio-demographic factors are assumed to be proxies for differences in taste for the arts, we do not understand the underlying determinants of tastes. Nor do we know what types of programming are likely to be most appealing to different tastes.

Finally, our review of the literature suggests that one key to deepening individuals' level of involvement with the arts is to instill in them a greater commitment to the arts so that the arts become central to who they are. But how to accomplish this remains unclear. Despite the best efforts of scores of institutions and dedicated individuals and the investment of uncounted dollars, participation building remains a very difficult and not very well understood task.

Inadequacy of Conceptual Approaches

Although these knowledge gaps may be frustrating to institutions attempting to design and implement participation-building strategies, they are probably inevitable. Neither policymakers nor practitioners are ever likely to have complete information on which to base their decisions. A more important—and potentially remediable—problem is the apparent failure of most theoretical approaches to capture the complexity of the process people go through in deciding whether to participate in the arts.

The empirical literature points out this complexity in several ways. For example, the very diversity of participation rates both by form of participation and type of art suggests that the factors driving these rates are not straightforward. Similarly, despite the prominence given to socio-demographic factors in most empirical studies of participation patterns, the literature suggests (as discussed earlier) that arts participation can be better explained if participants are sorted into three basic categories: those who participate rarely (if at all), occasionally, and frequently. Moreover, socio-demographic variables do not appear to be closely correlated with differences in frequency of participation once these three behavioral categories are distinguished from each other. In other words, although the more highly educated individuals are more likely than others to attend frequently, education appears to play little role in explaining why some frequent attenders attend so much more than others do (Schuster, 1991). Finally, the very diversity of the reasons individuals give for their decisions to participate suggests that the reasons are complex. Yet this complexity is not generally reflected in the theoretical literature, a fact that limits this literature's utility for practitioners.

Consider, for example, the fact that the theoretical literature implicitly treats the participation decision as dichotomous—i.e., as if one simply decided to participate or not participate. The diversity of responses that individuals give for their participation decisions suggests that this is not so, that people actually go through a series of different considerations when deciding whether to participate. They are likely, for example, to first consider whether the arts have anything to offer them. They then consider what those benefits are and where they are likely to find them. They might then consider different, specific opportunities to participate, such as attending a play or visiting an art museum. Finally, if they do end up participating, they are likely to evaluate their experience and subsequently revise (for better or worse) their initial expectations about the benefits of the arts.

We do not mean to suggest here that all individuals proceed in a linear fashion through all these steps. Much of the explanatory power of the behavioral distinction between rare, occasional, and frequent participants derives from the likelihood that these groups will be at different stages in the decisionmaking process. Frequent participants are already convinced that the arts are important to them and thus will focus on which events to choose. For those who are rare participants, consideration of which event to attend is not really relevant unless they somehow become convinced that the arts have something to offer them. A further complication in this decisionmaking process is introduced for individuals who participate not because of having come to a decision along the usual pathway but because a friend or relative has invited them to do so. Their decision may have less to do with the arts than with their relationship with the individual who invited them. Whether they participate in the future, however, will hinge at least in part on their participation experience.

The central point here is not the exact steps in the decisionmaking process but the fact that more than one decision is involved. Moreover, different factors are likely to determine the outcome of each of these decisions, and the influence of these factors is unlikely to be apparent if the process is not disaggregated. Perhaps the clearest example of why this disaggregation is important is the considerable variation found in the literature on how such economic constraints as ticket prices affect participation behavior. If, as we believe, ticket prices are only relevant for individuals already intending to attend, then estimating how prices will affect participation in the total population (as is implicitly done when a study regards participation as a dichotomous choice) will yield an inaccurate picture of pricing effects.

By oversimplifying the decision process, the theoretical literature fails to provide much guidance to arts institutions trying to decide which strategies to use to increase participation. In this context, the critical issue is determining which tactics are appropriate for which target populations (i.e., for those already participating, inclined to participate but not currently doing so, and not inclined to participate) and when to employ those tactics. For example, adjusting price levels in order to spur participation among individuals not inclined to participate in the first place, as many organizations do, is not likely to be very effective. An effective tactic in this case must deal with showing these people what benefits the arts offer them.

A second problem with the participation literature is its primary focus on objective, socio-demographic factors in explaining participation behavior.[9] As already noted, these do not explain why some individuals with a given set of background characteristics are frequent participants and others are not. This focus on socio-demographic factors rather than on the factors that motivate participants provides little help to arts institutions, since institutions typically have little or no way to influence background characteristics, including education.

Finally, by stressing socio-demographic factors, the conceptual models give too little attention to behavioral differences in participation, which in many ways seem to be the key to understanding participation decisions. In focusing on background factors, which institutions have little ability to modify, the conceptual models divert attention from contextual factors—e.g. how institutions advertise their message, the types of programming they offer, and the tactics they employ to increase participation—which institutions can modify.

---

[9]In our survey of arts organizations, most of them indicated that they identified target populations and designed strategies for those populations in terms of demographic characteristics alone.

The next chapter introduces a behavioral model of the decisionmaking process that we believe provides considerable insight into how and why individuals choose to participate and, as such, can help arts institutions attempting to design and implement effective participation-building strategies.

Chapter Three

A BEHAVIORAL MODEL OF PARTICIPATION

The model we created for this research is designed to provide a more complete understanding of the individual decisionmaking process than is currently available in the literature. It is specifically intended to help arts institutions gain a better understanding of that process and thus be able to influence people's participation decisions. It is predicated on the assumption that one must understand how the decisionmaking process actually works in order to influence people's behavior. If a behavioral model is to support efforts to influence behavior, it must do more than identify the factors correlated with a specific behavior. It must also specify how these factors operate.

The model recognizes that an individual's decision to take a specific action involves a complex mix of attitudes, intentions, constraints, and behaviors, as well as feedback between past experiences and the mix of attitudes and intentions.[1] It also recognizes that the arts participation decision is not simply a dichotomous behavior (to participate or not) but involves a complex set of considerations. The model tries to capture the complex dynamics of the decisionmaking process by incorporating the factors that may predispose an individual to act in a certain way; it also tries to identify how and at which stage of the process these factors come into play.

The key to our model is the recognition that there are several separate considerations, or stages, embedded in an individual's decisionmaking process and that different factors affect each stage. As described in Chapter Two, there are four stages: a general consideration of whether to consider the arts as a potential leisure activity (background stage), the formation of an inclination toward the arts based on an assessment of the benefits and costs of participation and where to obtain those benefits (stage 1), an evaluation of specific opportunities to participate (stage 2), and the actual arts experience followed by a reassess-

[1]We are indebted to Ann Stone, a Doctoral Fellow in policy analysis at the RAND Graduate School, whose insights helped us formulate this approach.

ment of the benefits and costs of the arts (stage 3). These stages link background factors to attitudes, attitudes to intentions, intentions to actual behavior, and past behavior to future behavior.

In addition, the model assumes that the effects of a particular set of factors on the decisionmaking process as a whole will be moderated by where those effects are most relevant to decisionmaking. As noted above, for example, to understand the effects of ticket prices on participation, it is important to focus not on all potential participants but on those already inclined to participate and thus likely to be at the stage in the decisionmaking process at which they care about the price of tickets. This point also helps to explain why it may be particularly important for an individual's initial experiences with the arts to be positive, since that experience can play a critical role in determining whether the individual is a repeat participant.

Figure 3.1 is a schematic of our participation model—i.e., the different stages an individual goes through in making participation decisions. As noted in Chapter Two, this is not to say that all individuals move self-consciously through the same process in deciding whether to participate in an arts program; instead, the model is meant to suggest important differences among people that can best be understood by recognizing that there are different components in the decisionmaking process. This distinction also helps make it clear that positive perceptions of the arts tend to precede any practical considerations about whether to attend a certain program or perform in an artistic event.

RAND*MR1323-3.1*

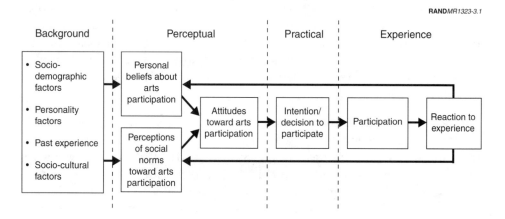

Figure 3.1—Participation Model

BACKGROUND STAGE

As Figure 3.1 shows, the model starts with an assessment of the set of background factors that shape an individual's general attitudes toward the arts. These factors, which reflect characteristics given prominence in the theoretical literature on participation, can be sorted into four categories:

- Socio-demographic factors—those describing an individual's social (education, income, occupation, etc.) and demographic (age, gender, life-cycle stage) characteristics.

- Personality factors—those that are unique to the individual.

- An individual's prior experiences with the arts.

- Socio-cultural factors—those describing an individual's group affiliations and identities.

At least initially, these background factors are exogenous to the participation decision because they are already established. Subsequent experience with the arts, however, can modify at least some of them, such as group identification or affiliation and prior experiences. Indeed, stage 3 of the model suggests that individuals will re-evaluate their attitudes toward arts participation based on their actual experiences.

PERCEPTUAL STAGE

Before considering whether to participate in a specific way, individuals are likely to assess the benefits and costs of arts participation and the different types of art and forms of participation they might choose. In other words, they must develop a predisposition, or inclination, to participate. These considerations will be influenced both by their attitudes toward the arts, including their perceptions of the benefits and costs of arts participation, and by their understanding of the social norms of their reference groups (relatives and friends) with respect to arts participation. The model recognizes that individuals' attitudes toward the arts are shaped both by their own beliefs and by the attitudes of the social groups with which they identify. It is possible, for example, that individuals personally predisposed toward the arts may not act on that predisposition because their reference groups would not consider it acceptable behavior. It could also happen that they participate not because they themselves are inclined to do so but because a friend or family member has brought them along. The relative importance of these two components in shaping an individual's overall inclination toward the arts will vary across individuals and groups and may well change over time.

The key point here is that an individual's attitudes toward the arts can predispose him or her either toward or against participation. An individual who is disinclined to participate will have a perceptual barrier that may be very difficult to overcome, regardless of what practical steps are taken to facilitate participation. Moreover, because these inclinations are based on individuals' personal beliefs about the benefits to be derived from the arts and their perceptions of how their reference groups perceive the arts, changing these inclinations can be very difficult and time consuming. In fact, changing an individual's inclinations may sometimes require changing the attitudes of his or her social groups.

An individual's inclination to participate will vary along a continuum from very strongly inclined to very strongly disinclined. The difficulty of getting someone to consider participating will vary according to the strength of his or her inclination and the form of participation. It will be easier to get arts aficionados, who are strongly inclined to participate, to consider participation than it will be to do so for casual attenders, who are much less inclined. In addition, because some forms of participation require very little effort (watching an arts program on television, listening to music on the radio), even those individuals who are only mildly inclined may be willing to give participation a try. Other forms of participation that involve considerably more effort (such as attending a concert, which might involve getting dressed up, traveling some distance, and being present for two to three hours), however, will require a greater inclination on the part of the individual.

Similarly, the efficacy of efforts to change individuals' inclinations by influencing their personal beliefs about the arts or those of their reference groups will vary depending on the strength of the individuals' inclinations and the degree of influence the reference groups wield over their behavior. In this context, it is important to recognize, as we suggested in Figure 2.1, that individuals may participate in the arts not just for the personal benefits they receive but also for the social experience. This social dimension can also affect the way in which individuals participate. For example, individuals who value the social aspects of arts participation may well be more inclined to attend concerts than those who do not value them.

Finally, how broadly one defines the arts affects the tally of people considered to be predisposed toward participation. For example, if popular music is included in the definition, then many more individuals will fall into the inclined category. Similarly, individual inclinations will vary across different types of art.

PRACTICAL STAGE

Individuals who have decided to become involved in the arts in some way have moved into the practical stage of the decisionmaking process and are ready to evaluate specific participation options. Even for these people, however, there are practical obstacles—lack of information about specific programs, high cost, lack of time, inconvenience, etc.—that must be addressed before they will actually participate at a specific time and place. Furthermore, the difficulty of overcoming these obstacles will depend on the strength of the person's inclination. People strongly inclined to participate are much less likely to be deterred by practical obstacles than are people only marginally inclined to participate. In fact, the strongly inclined are very likely to seek out extensive information on what is available, at what costs, and when. Those less strongly inclined, who will be more unfamiliar with the arts and thus more likely not to follow them on a regular basis, will not be as likely to seek out information, relying instead on word of mouth (referrals from friends and relatives) and the "buzz" surrounding specific events.

EXPERIENCE STAGE

If the practical barriers can be overcome, an individual will participate in a specific arts event and subsequently evaluate that experience. The arts experience can take several forms. Some individuals, for example, may choose to attend a performance or visit a museum. Others may decide to create art by studying to become an artist or working in some capacity in production (e.g., as a stagehand or selling tickets). The range of options will vary depending on the individual's familiarity with the arts and whether he or she has become part of an arts community, as suggested in Chapter Two. For those involved in a specific institution, the range is very likely to include serving as a volunteer, taking part in programming and outreach efforts, and contributing financially. These different modes of participation are not mutually exclusive; as the literature suggests, the more strongly predisposed individuals are toward the arts, the more likely they are to participate in multiple ways.

An individual's reaction to the experience will be influenced by a number of factors, including knowledge of the particular type of art, the value he or she gives to the social aspect of the experience, and the degree to which he or she derives personal fulfillment through the arts. Research has established that the better people understand an activity, the more likely they are to enjoy it (Kelley and Freisinger, 2000). Just as someone's enjoyment of a non-art form of leisure activity (say, a sport) increases with his or her understanding of that activity, so too does an individual's enjoyment of the arts increase as he or she knows more about them. As individuals become more familiar with and thus more knowledgeable about a particular type of art, their tastes are very likely to grow more varied and they will appreciate a wider range of programming.

Arts experiences can also have a social component. Many people are first introduced to the arts by their friends or family—often at an early age. Some individuals give high value to the social contacts afforded by the arts experience, and some find personal fulfillment and a sense of identity by connecting with a wider community of arts lovers (say, those who support a particular arts institution).

The opportunities that arts experiences provide for creativity, fulfillment, and personal meaning can also be a means of personal transformation for participants. This dimension of the experience, although difficult to measure, is an important factor in motivating individuals to deepen their participation, according to a recent study (Heinz Endowments, 1999) that identifies psychological themes people associate with the arts, such as the arts as "transporter" or "redeemer."

After individuals participate in an arts activity, their reaction to the experience then influences their subsequent decisions about whether to participate (as shown in Figure 3.1 by the arrows leading back to beliefs and perceptions). A particular arts experience can change individuals' expectations (for better or worse) about what the arts have to offer. It may also affect their receptivity (increasing or decreasing it) to their existing reference groups. It even can lead individuals to change their reference groups—for example, by increasing their identification with individuals who are more involved in the arts. As noted in Chapter Two, the most committed participants are likely to become immersed in a community of aficionados who view the arts (and perhaps a specific arts institution) as an essential component of their identity. Whether the outcome is positive or negative, the arts experience will feed back into the individual's overall experience, altering his or her attitudes and values and influencing future participation decisions. Frequent positive experiences can stimulate a person to participate more often and in more ways. Frequent participants are also more likely to participate in multiple art forms (Peters and Cherbo, 1996).

ADVANTAGES OF MODEL

Although our model is more elaborate than the standard theoretical approach, we recognize that it still cannot capture the full complexity of the decisionmaking process. Its value lies in its ability to reduce that complexity so as to arrive at a clearer understanding of the distinctions among types of influences on the decision and the effect of certain sets of factors on others. As long as the model avoids serious distortions of the decisionmaking process, it can serve a number of useful purposes.

The advantage of the model's way of describing participation is that it can help organizations develop more targeted—and therefore more effective—initiatives for encouraging participation. By recognizing that individuals can be grouped according to their stage within the participation decisionmaking process—and that different types of obstacles to participation are associated with each stage—the model can help institutions identify the tactics that will address the obstacles most relevant to their target group. Each stage of the decisionmaking process provides guidance for developing effective institutional strategies.

Chapter Four

DEVELOPING STRATEGIES AND TACTICS

The principal advantage of our model over more traditional approaches is that it can help organizations develop more targeted—and therefore more effective—strategies for increasing public participation in their activities. The key point of the model's effectiveness is the recognition that individuals may be at very different stages of the decisionmaking process, that different factors drive decisions at each of these stages, and thus that the tactics used to influence behavior must be appropriate for the stage of the target population. This chapter develops this point and its implications for developing effective engagement strategies and tactics.

ALIGNING GOALS, TARGET POPULATIONS, AND TACTICS

During our site visits and in our survey, we asked organizations about the tactics they used to build participation.[1] These questions covered a variety of tactics, including what they did to learn about current and potential participants and how they publicized their activities. Despite some variation, the vast majority of these organizations relied on the same basic battery of tactics. The most striking finding of this research, in fact, was the similarity of the methods used.[2] This finding is not particularly surprising, since the range of tactics arts organizations have at their disposal for accomplishing these tasks is not extensive. What is important about this finding is that it suggests that the central issue organizations face in designing engagement strategies is deciding which available tactics are appropriate for different target populations and when they should be used.

Our model provides a way to decide which tactics to use by recognizing the connections among three central elements of the participation process: how

---

[1]Appendix B describes the participation-building results of the survey.

[2]The results of these comparisons are displayed in Appendix B, Figure B.2 and Tables B.10 and B.12.

organizations plan to increase participation, where their target populations are in the process of deciding whether to participate in the arts, and what types of factors are relevant to each position in the participation decisionmaking process. Table 4.1 shows how these different elements align.

As noted in Chapter One, organizations can build participation in three ways:

- They can *diversify* participation by attracting different kinds of people than they already attract.

- They can *broaden* participation by attracting more people.

- They can *deepen* participation by increasing their current participants' levels of involvement.

As Table 4.1 indicates, in our model each participation goal is appropriate for a specific target population. And the specific target population determines which factors are relevant in devising effective tactics. Thus, for example, efforts to diversify participation are most appropriate for individuals not inclined to participate. These people believe the arts are not likely to be of benefit to them and thus must be persuaded of the benefits they could derive from participation—i.e., they are at the stage in the decisionmaking process where perceptual factors are most relevant.

Efforts to broaden participation, however, are most appropriate for individuals already inclined to participate but not currently doing so. These individuals must be provided with information on what types of programs are available, when, and at what prices, and on why these programs might interest them. In other words, this group is at the stage of the process where practical factors are most relevant.

Finally, efforts to deepen participation are most appropriate for individuals currently participating. For these people, the challenge is to convince them to become more involved, which means making their participation more rewarding. The key goals here are to increase these people's knowledge of the art form relevant to them and to instill in them a sense of belonging to the institution's community. In other words, this group is at the stage where the experience factors are most relevant.

Table 4.1

Alignment Among Goals, Target Populations, and Relevant Factors

Participation goal	Diversify	Broaden	Deepen
Target population	Disinclined	Inclined	Current participants
Relevant factors	Perceptual	Practical	Experience

EFFECTIVE TACTICS ARE TARGETED TACTICS

By suggesting how the different elements of the participation process are related, our model provides a basis for deciding which strategies and tactics an arts organization should use for the three different groups of participants.

To increase participation among people not inclined to participate—i.e., to *diversify* participation—the greatest challenge is to overcome the perceptual barriers and change their attitudes toward the arts. As long as these people view the arts as exclusive, elite, abstract, or otherwise not related to their lives, they will not consider participating. The aim here is thus to make them see the arts as accessible, tangible, and more closely related to their everyday lives. Specific outreach tactics might include programming that relates to their particular interests, sending artists into their communities to discuss art, and helping them recognize the continuum between entertainment forms they may be familiar with (e.g., commercial films, religious music) and the more traditional nonprofit arts (e.g., theater and music). To reach this group, organizations may need to send representatives to non-arts venues where these individuals spend their time and feel comfortable. Another tactic is to emphasize the social aspects of the arts, which might entail approaching individuals through their own social groups and emphasizing the opportunities the arts offer for social interaction.

To increase participation among the population inclined to participate but not currently doing so—i.e., to *broaden* participation—the key is to overcome the existing practical barriers. The main barrier for this group is likely to be lack of information about an organization's programs and what they offer. Other barriers are inconvenience of the programs, high prices, lack of access to program venues, and childcare problems.[3] The aim here is to understand the lifestyles of these people and to adjust accordingly. Getting the needed information to these people may involve first determining the channels they use to get information (the media; personal recommendations from friends, relatives, or community groups; presentations at workplaces, direct mailings, etc.) and the types of messages best for reaching them (messages that emphasize aspects likely to resonate with particular age or ethnic groups or that highlight the creative aspects of the arts). Similarly, to help overcome the practical barriers to this population's participation, program schedules and locations might be varied, transportation provided, and programs and activities priced more affordably.

To increase the level of involvement of current participants—i.e., to *deepen* participation—the key is to make the arts experiences of these individuals as

---

[3]All of these barriers were cited by the organizations contacted. See, for example, Appendix B, Tables B.8 and B.9.

rewarding as possible. One tactic for doing this is to increase this population's knowledge about the arts by providing special events, seminars, workshops, and pre- and post-performance discussions. Another tactic is to enhance the social dimension of the arts experience by offering social events before or after programs, the aim being to develop in these people a sense of belonging to a community.

Arts organizations that focus only on the population already participating or on the population not participating but inclined to do so exclude the largest pool of possible participants: the population not even actively considering participation. The general attitude toward the arts of this group, which is in the background stage of our model's decisionmaking process, is influenced by a variety of background factors, such as socio-demographic and personality characteristics, prior arts experiences (or lack thereof), and group affiliations and identities—all factors over which institutions typically have very little leverage. However, the model suggests that background factors be viewed not as individuals' fixed inheritances from the past but, rather, as points of connection between arts organizations and potential participants.

Taking this view, arts organizations must look for ways to penetrate the "awareness space" of these individuals. One possible approach is to reach out to them through their family or friends. Organizations might, for example, encourage current participants to bring friends and relatives when they attend an event and offer discounts when they do. They might also offer programs in which children learn various forms of artistic expression and which subsequently draw family members into the population of participants (say, as an audience for their children's performances). In reaching out in ways such as these, an organization becomes a community itself, one with influence over the attitudes and values of potential participants.

Another tactic is to conduct active outreach programs with key community organizations, such as schools and churches, to foster arts programs that will help children and their families develop positive attitudes toward the arts. Organizations can also go to workplaces and public meeting spaces in the community to publicly display their art in an effort to raise awareness both of the arts in general and of their specific offerings. Subsequent to such community outreach efforts, institutions should follow up with the individuals contacted to encourage them to consider more active involvement with the arts.

INFORMATION IS CRITICAL TO THE ENGAGEMENT PROCESS

As this discussion suggests, information is critical to the design and implementation of effective engagement strategies. This information must flow in two directions: from potential and current participants to arts organizations and from arts organizations to potential and current participants. Arts organizations, for example, need various types of information about target populations if they are to design and implement effective engagement strategies. Similarly, potential and current participants need information about arts organizations and their offerings if they are to make informed choices.

Information Organizations Need About Participants

An effective participation-building strategy is a targeted strategy, and three types of information are important to arts organizations attempting to build a targeted strategy. First, since one key to devising such a strategy is understanding where the target population is in the participation decisionmaking process, an arts organization must find out what its target populations' inclinations toward the arts are. Most organizations can distinguish between those who currently participate and those who do not, but this distinction alone is not sufficient. They must also be able to differentiate nonparticipants who are inclined to participate from nonparticipants who are not so inclined. This distinction is important because the tactics devised to influence the groups' decisions need to be different (i.e., they must aim at different factors).

The second type of information concerns people who are inclined to participate. People in this group consider many issues before actually deciding to participate (what form their participation should take, what discipline it should involve, which institution to choose, etc.), so devising an effective strategy for attracting these people requires information about their motivations (e.g., whether they are looking for entertainment or enrichment, and whether they are more likely to prefer self-focused or social activities).

An understanding of the relevant motivations can help arts organizations identify which individuals are likely to be inclined toward their organization and how best to convey their message, and thus is useful in devising a strategy. In addition, the issue of artistic mission comes into play. Organizations do not all emphasize the same artistic missions. Some emphasize the creative aspect of their art form by stressing training and creativity and putting the individual participant at the center of their activities. These types of organizations may be particularly appealing to individuals who are more interested in hands-on activities—e.g., those who are self-focused and oriented toward enrichment and fulfillment (see Chapter Two's discussion of motivations). Other organizations focus on the arts as a vehicle for enhancing communities. For them, stressing the social aspects of participation may be more appropriate. Still other organizations are primarily interested in promoting the canons of specific art forms by fostering an appreciation of their art. For these organizations, the potential audience may well consist of two types of participants—casual attenders and aficionados—which means they may need different appeals for these two groups.

Third, and finally, arts organizations need specific information about the lifestyles, specific program interests, and leisure activities of potential participants and how these groups stay informed about their leisure activities. With this information, arts organizations will be able to adapt their programming, scheduling, pricing, and marketing efforts to the specific needs of the potential audiences.

The types of information just described may be correlated with the kinds of traditional socio-demographic data often available from marketing organizations, but none is directly demographic per se. Rather, these types of information describe the attitudes, inclinations, motivations, and tastes of potential participants. This difference is important, because when we asked the organizations in our survey to describe their target populations, over three-quarters of them defined those populations in socio-demographic rather than behavioral or attitudinal terms.[4]

It is interesting to compare the three types of information we see as important to participation-building strategies with what the arts organizations we surveyed reported about their current and target populations and the methods they used to obtain that information.[5] As might be expected, these organizations reported that they knew considerably more about their current participants than about their target populations. Although almost two-thirds of them said they knew very much or much about their current participants, only about one-third said they knew an equivalent amount about their target populations. Conversely, while close to one-quarter knew "little" or "nothing at all" about their target populations, less than 5 percent knew little or nothing about current participants.

As for how the institutions obtained this information, they told us they used several informal and formal techniques: discussions with staff, with advisory committees, and with community members (informal); and surveys, focus groups, and other traditional marketing means (formal). The organizations were far more likely to use informal than formal techniques to learn about participants, and each of the three informal methods was used more frequently than any one of the formal methods. The most frequently used informal method was discussions among staff. Using informal methods like these to gather information on current and potential participants may well limit an or-

---

[4]This point is described in Appendix B, Table B.4.

[5]The information presented here is discussed more fully in Appendix B and displayed in Table B.6 and Figures B.2 and B.3.

ganization's ability to measure the kinds of behavioral and attitudinal factors needed to develop effective engagement strategies. And the most frequently used formal method, surveys (used between a fair amount and much of the time), most often provided information only on current participants.

Information Participants Need About Organizations

Just as arts organizations need information about current and potential participants, so too do participants need information about arts organizations and what they have to offer. The types of information participants need, however, vary depending on where the individuals are in the decisionmaking process. For individuals not inclined to participate in the arts, the key challenge is to convince them of the arts' benefits to them. These people thus need information that makes them conscious of the arts and their benefits. One tactic for reaching these people might be to frame the institution's message in terms of the advantages offered by the arts compared with other leisure activities.

For people inclined to participate but not currently doing so, the challenge is to convince them to sample the organization's offerings. To meet this challenge, organizations need to provide basic information about the activities they offer, including when, where, and at what price. In addition, they need to market their activities in a way that persuades individuals to participate—i.e., by linking the activities to potential participants' specific interests.

Finally, for those already participating, the challenge is to convince them to increase their level of involvement. The key here is to make the participation experience as enjoyable and rewarding as possible by increasing these individuals' understanding and knowledge of the arts

How to Convey Information to Potential and Current Participants

Focusing on the information needs of the three different groups is only part of the information picture. The effectiveness of outreach strategies hinges on both the substance of the message conveyed and how that message is delivered. Information channels differ, not only in their ability to reach different populations but also in terms of their credibility. We have no a priori reason to differentiate among information channels along these dimensions, but we did ask the organizations we surveyed to describe how they communicated with current and potential participants and how effective these communication efforts were. We did not ask these organizations to distinguish among our three types of participants, however, so our results make no distinctions as to intended audiences.

Our survey results indicate that the interviewed arts organizations place a high priority on publicizing their activities and use a combination of resources for this task. We asked them about their use of ten techniques: word of mouth, free media, direct mail, presentations to community groups, community collabora- tors, handouts, paid media, the Internet, personal telephone calls, and bill- boards. Seven of the 10 were used by almost 90 percent of the organizations, and no technique was used by fewer than 50 percent.[6] Every organization relied on word of mouth and free media publicity, almost all used direct mail, and be- tween 80 and 95 percent used presentations to community groups, community collaborators, handouts, paid advertisements in the media, and the Internet. The two least popular techniques were personal telephone calls and billboards.

There was considerably less agreement about the effectiveness of these differ- ent techniques. Word of mouth and direct mail were rated as the two most highly effective techniques, yet they were rated as highly effective by only 40 percent of the organizations. Interestingly, both of these techniques rely on an already established link between the organization and its participants. Word of mouth relies on contacts among family and friends of potential participants, and direct mailings are sent out to those who either have already participated at an institution or are on a mailing list obtained from another organization (and thus might be expected to have participated there). Free media publicity in the form of general interest stories about the organization or its programs in the local press and paid advertising were also rated as being effective by a substan- tial number of organizations.

These comparisons suggest that there is a discrepancy between the importance our model ascribes to the two-way exchange of information between art organi- zations and potential and current participants and what the arts organizations we surveyed said about their information collection and dissemination tactics. By and large, the organizations were much more likely to rely on informal than formal techniques to collect information about participants, and of those in- formal techniques, discussions among staff were used the most. This may well explain why these organizations generally knew much more about their current participants than about their target populations. Moreover, it is unclear whether these informal techniques are well suited to collecting the attitudinal and behavioral information about participants that is essential to developing effective engagement strategies.

These comparisons also raise questions about how arts organizations deliver their message to current and potential participants. These organizations clearly understood the importance of conveying their message to potential partici-

---

[6]The results of our comparisons are reported in Appendix B, Table B.10.

pants, but their effectiveness in doing this is unclear. Despite the fact that these institutions used a wide variety of techniques, no more than at best 40 percent of them rated these techniques as effective in delivering their message. Given the diversity of their approaches, we suspect that the problem does not lie in the delivery channels they use per se but, rather, in knowing when to use the channels and for which groups. As our model suggests, the key to effective information dissemination is to understand the behavior and attitudes of the target audience and to tailor the tactics used accordingly. If arts institutions lack a firm understanding of these characteristics, they will not be positioned to develop the right message, regardless of the channels they choose for its delivery.

Chapter Five

THE NEED FOR AN INTEGRATIVE APPROACH

Chapter Four focuses on the specific strategies and tactics organizations might use to build participation based on their participation goals and target populations. But arts organizations also need to consider how building participation fits with their overall purpose and mission, their available resources, and the community environment in which they operate. Given their resource constraints and competing organizational interests, arts organizations must consider all of these factors.

To balance all these considerations requires an integrative approach, one that begins with the assumption that all of an organization's key activities should serve its ultimate purpose. Before selecting participation goals and the tactics to use to achieve them, organizations should re-examine their purpose and mission, consider what priority to assign to their different institutional goals, and determine how participation building aligns with their ultimate organizational purpose.[1]

Not all organizations do this. Some take a more tactical approach, first selecting specific participation goals and then choosing tactics by which to achieve those goals and establishing priorities for the goals as a way to direct scarce resources. Setting such priorities and resolving conflicts among multiple stakeholders are challenging tasks in any case, but especially if organizations have not considered how increasing participation supports the organization's basic purpose and mission. As Cyert and March (1963) note, many organizations react to competing demands either via a patchwork of separate actions, first going in one direction, then another; or by trying to meet all demands at the same time, risking failure in the process.

---

[1] As discussed in Appendix A, organizations with different purposes tend to emphasize different participation goals, choose different target populations, and focus on different tactics for increasing participation.

This chapter elaborates on the steps involved in taking an integrative approach to building participation and provides specific examples of how institutions have approached these steps. Our purpose is not to propose a single strategy or set of best practices for increasing participation. We believe that organizations should build participation in ways specifically tailored to their own circumstances, so what we offer is a process that can be applied in different institutional contexts.

STEPS IN AN INTEGRATIVE APPROACH

An integrative approach to building participation involves several steps:

- Linking an organization's participation-building activities to its core values and purpose by choosing participation goals that support that purpose.

- Identifying clear target groups and basing its tactics on good information about those groups.

- Understanding the internal and external resources that can be committed to building participation.

- Establishing a process for feedback and self-evaluation.

Linking Participation-Building Activities to Core Values and Purpose

The first step is essentially equal to putting the organization's purpose at the center of the process of developing participation goals. Successful programs require the commitment of all key staff and operating units of an organization, the board, and the network of funders. Such shared commitment must be based on the conviction that sustained audience development is critical to achieving the organization's mission. The organization must articulate a clear set of participation goals that serve its basic purpose and mission and around which it can build consensus. Without this link, participation-building activities may be perceived as serving multiple, conflicting purposes or, even worse, as marginal to the institution's real work.

One of the major challenges facing many of the institutions we visited was how to get staff and board members united behind a common set of participation goals. Addressing this challenge often required that the institution's mission be re-examined and the way in which the mission would be furthered by the participation goals be spelled out. Even when there was agreement on the participation goals, they sometimes were at odds with other institutional goals. For example, several organizations said that resistance surfaced among some staff and existing groups of participants when programs to attract new participants were initiated.

The goal-setting process needs to begin with a consideration of the organization's purpose and mission (Shortell and Kaluzny, 1994). The important question at this early point is, How do the participation goals support the organization's basic purpose?

While virtually all of the organizations we contacted had mission statements, few had explicit statements of purpose. Purpose and mission are related but different. An organization's purpose answers the question, Why does this organization exist? Its mission answers the question, What does this organization want to achieve? (Bart, 1986).

To clarify this distinction, consider the following analogy from the world of sports. Baseball is played at several levels. At the top are major league teams, below them are several levels of minor leagues, and below these are various levels of amateur teams. There are similar team activities (or missions) at all levels. No matter what the level, for example, all teams play the same game, try to win, draw support from fans, and usually promote the communities in which they are located. However, the ultimate purpose of their activities differs. In the major leagues, the ultimate goal is likely to be earning a profit; in the minor leagues (e.g., rookie leagues funded by major league teams), the ultimate goal is to develop individual talent capable of moving up to the major leagues; and at the amateur level, the ultimate goal is likely to be the enjoyment of the participants. These differences in purpose influence a wide variety of decisions affecting how teams are organized and what priorities they attach to their different activities or missions.[2].

Our research revealed that the institutions we surveyed can be classified into three broad types according to their underlying purpose:

- Organizations chiefly dedicated to supporting the canons of specific art forms.

- Organizations chiefly dedicated to improving their communities using art as a vehicle.

- Organizations serving as centers of creativity and chiefly dedicated to training new artists and engaging individuals in the creative process.

These distinctions represent "ideal types" for purposes of illustration. We recognize, for example, that arts organizations cannot be neatly categorized as having a single purpose; nor will their participation goals be determined exclusively by these factors. All of the arts organizations we contacted were committed to furthering their art form, improving their community, and enhancing the lives

---

[2]Examples of this distinction between purpose and mission are contained in Appendix A.

of their participants. However, the priorities they attached to these purposes did differ and were often reflected in their participation goals and approaches. To clarify these differences in priorities, the following paragraphs summarize information drawn from some of our site visits.

We found that organizations whose emphasis was on furthering the canons of a particular art form placed the art form at the center of their activities. As such, their greatest emphasis was on fostering an appreciation of their art form, providing opportunities for the public to experience their art, preserving and collecting existing works of arts, creating new art, and other such activities. Like all arts organizations, they were interested in increasing their participants' involvement with their art form at all levels, but their initial emphasis was on giving individuals more exposure to their art as viewers and audience members—that is, as traditional consumers rather than as active creators. They thus tended to place higher priority on broadening and diversifying participation rather than on deepening it. In fact, increasing participation was often viewed as a vehicle for increasing the range of individuals who value the art form and improving the institution's image as a valued and respected supplier of art.

Organizations emphasizing the use of art as a vehicle for improving the community placed the community at the center of their activities. They sought not only to improve the community through art, but to increase their community's involvement with art; to provide more community members with the opportunity to experience art; and to stress the societal, community, and other benefits of the arts. Since these institutions view the arts as a vehicle for engagement, they tended to place high priority on deepening current participation and diversifying participation to include members of the community not currently engaged in the arts. Increasing participation in both of these ways is central to their community-based mission; it also serves to validate their legitimacy within the community and is a necessary condition for fulfillment of their mission.

Organizations emphasizing creativity and the creation of new art were likely to place the individual at the center of their activities. Thus, they tended to concentrate on training artists, involving individuals in the creative process, and creating new art. Because they seek to transform individuals by involving them with the creative process, they tended to emphasize deepening rather than broadening or diversifying. Indeed, arts organizations focused on creativity often try to create a one-to-one personal connection with the individual. Since the level of involvement these institutions hope to achieve often requires great commitment and trust between the organization and its participants, participants are often included in the strategic planning process.

Identifying Target Groups and Developing Tactics Based on Good Information

Once the participation goals have been chosen, the next step is to decide on an operational plan for reaching those goals. This task involves deciding which target populations to choose, how to gather information about them, and what tactics to employ based on this knowledge. These tactical decisions involve how to gather and analyze information about the target group, what kinds of programming might attract this specific population, how best to inform the target group of the institution's offerings, where and when to best schedule programs and other offerings for this group. The institution must also decide how the operational plan fits with the organization's current activities.

Identifying Target Groups. Before an organization chooses its target population, it should look at what it considers to be its community, or service area. It makes little sense for an institution to choose a target population not represented in its service area. The organizations we visited defined their communities of service in different ways. Some clearly defined them in primarily *geographic* terms. For example, Hancher Auditorium and Ballet Arizona focused their efforts on entire states; the Cleveland Museum of Art and the St. Louis Symphony Orchestra focused their efforts on metropolitan areas. Others, such as Freedom Theatre, Cal Arts, and Old Town School of Folk Music, defined their service communities mainly in terms of specific *demographic* groups. Still others, such as The Loft and Poet's House, defined their service communities primarily in terms of people who share a particular *behavioral* characteristic, such as people who write or who love poetry. By identifying its service community, an organization can narrow the range of options it needs to consider in selecting a target population.

Within any service community, however, there will be a wide range of populations that could be targeted. Organizations may use several different "prisms" to help narrow their choices. They might, for example, consider which group is the most underserved within their community or which is growing most rapidly. Or they might consider which of the three forms of participation is most important to their purpose and mission and choose their target population accordingly. For example, an organization focused on broadening participation might decide on a target population that appears to be interested in the arts but is not currently involved in its activities. And an organization focused on deepening participation might choose to target a group it believes is interested in being directly involved in the creative process. Organizations might also consider how well-aligned their current activities are with the interests of their target population. For example, an organization that offers educational classes to school-age children might consider targeting parents, since those classes already provide a natural bridge to parental involvement.

Learning About Target Groups. Once an organization has identified its target population, it then needs to gather information about that group. As noted in Chapter Four, organizations use various techniques for this purpose, such as surveys, focus groups, interviews, and discussions with knowledgeable community members. Whatever technique is used, information gathering is a crucial step. Institutions that identify how target populations view the arts, why they might be interested in participating, and what they consider to be major obstacles to their participation are more likely to succeed in reaching new audiences. When the Cleveland Museum of Art launched a major community-engagement initiative to reach underserved populations, it began by forming a committee to help identify and target such groups and to design outreach efforts likely to appeal to them.

To choose tactics that will be effective in reaching target groups, organizations must know something both about why those groups might be inclined to participate in the arts and about the perceptual, practical, and experience barriers that may make them reluctant to act on their inclinations. Appendix B documents the fact that arts organizations identify many reasons why individuals may be interested in the arts. Some individuals are intrinsically interested in the arts in general or in a particular type of art; other individuals are attracted by the opportunity the arts provide to be part of a wider community of people sharing a common experience. Still other people are motivated by the desire to express themselves artistically or find the arts enriching; others want their families to experience the arts. Most individuals are motivated by more than one reason when they decide to engage in an arts activity. Understanding what these motivations might be and how they fit with the organization's current programs is critical to developing effective participation-building tactics.

Developing Appropriate Tactics. To address the *perceptual* barriers a target group might have, many organizations we interviewed developed programs and activities specifically designed to change their public image. The Cleveland Museum of Art, for example, introduced several new initiatives designed to counter its image as an "elite" institution and to broaden its appeal within the community. These initiatives included a program to bring 20 art exhibits a year into shopping centers, schools, and community centers; community-oriented programming that set aside specific days for target groups to come to the museum; informal barbecues twice a week at the museum; and an annual Mardi Gras-style parade that involved workshops on float and costume design located throughout the community. The St. Louis Symphony Orchestra instituted a community partnership program to send small groups of musicians into schools, churches, and civic organizations to perform and discuss their music.

Ballet Arizona added a "Dias de Los Muertos" program to attract Hispanic participants and mythology programs to attract Native American audiences.

As for the *practical* factors, organizations need to consider those aspects of the target group's lifestyle that will influence participation in their programs, such as how these individuals learn about cultural events and what times will best fit their schedules. Many organizations we interviewed relied on community leaders (including representatives of sports clubs) in publicizing their activities and convened community advisory councils for special events and exhibits. Some institutions advertised their activities in Spanish and other languages; others expanded their operating hours to include nights and weekends so as to fit more people's schedules. Still others offered discounts or special coupons to attract certain participants.

The *experience* factors that must be considered are the target group's reaction to the programs and the institution's atmosphere. Many organizations are trying different ways to create a more receptive environment, such as training and evaluating staff on their willingness to serve visitors, holding pre- and post-program talks to increase participants' understanding of and familiarity with the arts, and providing opportunities for visitors to socialize in conjunction with arts events. For example, in opening a restaurant in its new facility, Old Town School of Folk Music sought not only to raise revenues but also to make its atmosphere more comfortable and inviting, to create an opportunity to inform visitors about upcoming events, and to offer an informal place to meet and talk with visitors.

Understanding the Organization's Resources

Once an organization has selected its participation goals and tactics, it needs to determine the resources that will be necessary to implement its participation-building strategy and how they will be obtained. This step requires the organization to take stock of its own resources in light of other institutional demands, which entails assessing all internal assets (staff, professional abilities, facilities, and equipment) and resources available in the broader community.

Understanding Internal Resources. All organizations have certain basic institutional needs: hiring, training, and motivating staff; operating within budgets; self-governance; and adapting to change. Balancing the resources allocated to these various needs with those required to implement participation-building strategies can lead to tensions within the organization. In our surveys, some organizational leaders talked about tensions between those concerned with controlling expenditures on production costs and those wanting to develop programs that would appeal to a broad range of participants. Others mentioned tensions between marketing staff and creative directors over whether to develop programs that appeal to existing versus potential participants.

In fact, concerns about friction over how programs designed to appeal to new audiences would affect existing audiences were not at all uncommon. This friction arose within the staff and sometimes between boards and staff—especially if there were already disagreements regarding the importance of building participation or the emphasis assigned to certain participation goals. Growing organizations seem to have a greater potential for such conflicts. Several of the institutions referred to the need to maintain communication and "a sense of connectedness" among the staff when an organization is growing.

Internal tensions were often different depending on organization size. Large organizations in our survey, for example, often had more resources and expertise but sometimes found it difficult to get staff committed to the organization's participation goals. In small organizations, tensions often arose over the increased workload required to build participation. Responsibility for implementing strategies and building collaborative relationships with other groups tended to fall on staff who were already overcommitted, leading several small arts organizations to use their grant funds to add staff and expertise to deal with the extra duties.

The resources that an organization needs to implement its participation strategies are not limited to dollars and staff time and abilities. They also include less tangible resources, such as leadership, knowledge of target populations, and visibility and reputation in the community. Although more resources are generally preferred to fewer resources, the organizations recognized that resources considered to be assets in working with one target population could actually be a liability in working with another. For example, prestige within the community and a reputation as an elite institution may help an organization broaden the participation of individuals inclined toward the arts, but they may also serve as a barrier for those who see the institution as elitist and thus not for people like them. Many institutions noted the importance of changing their image within the community and establishing trust between themselves and their target groups.

Collaborating with Other Organizations. Virtually all the organizations we contacted recognized the importance of establishing strategic alliances with other institutions and individuals within the community as a way to expand available resources. Some of these alliances were through long-established collaborations, and some were set up for specific projects or programs. Many of the organizations noted, for example, that they had established community advisory committees to help them develop programs and reach out to target populations. Collaborations with artists, arts organizations, and other community organizations were also frequently developed to further participation goals.

Two particularly interesting approaches to community collaborations are the Poet's House "Poetry in the Branches" program and The Loft's collaboration with other literary organizations. Poet's House collaborates with the New York Public Library to advise librarians on how to build a good poetry collection, create poetry displays, and foster broader appreciation of poetry through writing workshops and poetry readings. The Loft has an agreement with several other literary organizations—a bookbinding and paper-making center (The Minnesota Center for Book Art), a small press (Milkweed Editions), and a bookstore (The Hungry Mind)—to share space in the same building.

Although community collaborations are central to most organizations' participation-building tactics, establishing a successful alliance is not an easy task, according to what we were told. The long-term effect of such collaborations may be to expand the resources available to an organization, but their development is a time-intensive process and may in the short term create more costs than benefits. Arts organizations emphasized that for collaborations to work, the missions of the collaborating organizations must be complementary and the expectations and the assets each party brings to the effort must be made explicit.

Establishing a Feedback and Evaluation Process

The overall task of developing participation goals and operational plans and allocating resources is unlikely to be straightforward. Organizations are apt to begin with an initial planning phase, start the implementation process, and then revisit earlier decisions armed with what they have learned from actual experiences. The final step in an integrative approach thus is to establish a process for evaluation and feedback. A thorough process for evaluating both operational plans and the progress being made in implementing them should be built in so that activities can be adjusted as the participation-building program proceeds. Such a process also assures that enough information is collected from the outset so that the organization can assess its own performance and communicate the results to various stakeholders. Moreover, such a process helps organizations realize that developing a successful program takes time and requires both sustained commitment and a willingness to modify the approach as warranted.

Often this process begins with a strategic planning exercise in which the organization's staff and board re-examine the organizational purpose and mission before they even begin to choose a set of goals and tactics. As the leadership of the Walker Arts Center explained, the development of a plan was critical to their efforts: "We spent lots of time working on our plan and developed a sense of "mantra" about it—it formed our marching orders." Beginning with this type of exercise can be an essential first step, but the resulting initial plans need to be revisited, and often they need to be modified.

Organizations adopting an integrative approach to participation-building thus need to incorporate an evaluation and feedback process. A key element of the evaluation process is development of a set of measures that can be used as a benchmark in assessing progress. Virtually all of the organizations we visited described different criteria they had used to assess the success of their participation-building efforts.

In choosing these yardsticks, the organizations considered two important questions: What do we mean by success? And how do we measure it? Nearly every one of these institutions looked to changes in patterns of participation as measures of success, but many also considered a broader range of indicators that provided insight into how participation affected the organization's broader goals. Whether they focused just on changes in participation patterns or also looked at success more broadly, these organizations believed that success could not be measured strictly in quantitative terms. All of them also considered a range of qualitative measures of how well they were doing. The following discussion provides examples of how the organizations approached these evaluation tasks.

When we asked the organizations how they measured the success of their participation-building efforts, virtually all of them mentioned changes in the number of participants—but this was typically just the starting point. How they measured the changes varied depending on whether the organization focused on increasing attendance (measured in number of attendees and box office receipts), involving participants in various training programs (measured in enrollments), or increasing circulation (for example, Poet's House, which initiated a poetry outreach effort in the New York Public Library, looked at numbers of books of poetry in circulation). Most organizations also measured changes in their participants' diversity, which entailed paying attention to the demographics of new participants and how they compared with those of prior participants and with the composition of the community. To gauge the extent to which current participants had become more deeply involved, some institutions collected information on the frequency of repeat attendance and return visits, and the degree to which occasional participants were converted to subscribers or volunteers. Sometimes this entailed upgrading record systems to keep better track of participation.

Although the organizations all used quantitative measures to capture certain effects of their efforts, they all were adamant that some important effects could be adequately captured only through more qualitative measures. Some assessed participants' reactions to specific programs, including their level of engagement and level of comfort with the experience. Others looked for the degree to which the participants knew and interacted with the staff and vice versa, the number of hits on the organization's Web site, how long individuals had been involved with the organization, or the level of community involvement with the organization, including the number of people who wanted to work at the organization.

Many organizations also noticed the effects that participation building had on other aspects of their operations. They reported that building participation often contributed to broader institutional goals, such as those concerning staff morale, board involvement, and the quality and diversity of the programs they were able to offer. Several organizations, for example, mentioned the positive effects their participation efforts had on the morale of staff and artists with whom they worked. As staff and artists became more involved with participants and the communities these institutions served, their enthusiasm and satisfaction grew. Other organizations noted that their board became more involved with their work as a result of the participation initiatives. Still others mentioned that increasing participation levels helped their efforts to attract artists to work with them, which expanded both the range and the complexity of the programs they could offer.

Two other indirect benefits of participation-building activities were mentioned by several organizations: they received more media coverage, and they had greater success in raising funds. Since lack of visibility and inadequate funding were rated as significant problems by many organizations, these two consequences were considered very important, not only to the success of their participation initiatives but also to fulfilling their institutional mission.

* * * * *

In sum, an integrative approach to building participation requires that arts organizations do more than just focus on their participation-building activities. They must also consider how those activities align with the institution's purpose and mission and its available resources, as well as how that alignment will affect other organizational goals and activities. Moreover, they need to evaluate their participation-building efforts as they progress, modifying their activities as appropriate.

Chapter Six

SUMMARY AND CONCLUSIONS

This final chapter presents our conclusions, assembled from the previous chapters, about how arts institutions might best go about their efforts to build public participation in their activities. The salient points concerning effective strategies and the need for an integrative approach are recapped. Also provided is a recap of the guidelines arts organizations should keep in mind as they design and implement their engagement strategies.

EFFECTIVE ENGAGEMENT STRATEGIES

Effective engagement strategies are targeted strategies. The key to developing such strategies is knowing what tactics to use with which target populations and when. The alignment of participation goals, target populations, and participation-building tactics is central to this process. Each of the ways to increase participation—by broadening it, deepening it, or diversifying it—is best suited to a different population depending on where that population is in the process of deciding whether to participate in the arts. Broadening is best suited to individuals already inclined to participate in the arts but not presently doing so (i.e., infrequent participants); deepening is most appropriate for those already involved with the arts (frequent participants); diversifying is appropriate for individuals not inclined to participate in the arts (rare, if ever, participants). Recognizing the distinctions among these different groups and that certain tactics are appropriate for each group is the primary challenge in developing effective engagement strategies.

Information is essential to the alignment of goals, target populations, and tactics, and it must flow both from potential and current participants to arts organizations and from arts organizations to potential and current participants. Arts organizations cannot properly align their goals with their target populations and tactics if they do not have accurate information about those populations. And this information must be more than the socio-demographic data routinely collected by many organizations; it must also cover the attitudes, lifestyles, leisure behavior, motivations, and specific program interests of their target populations, as well as any potential barriers that might inhibit these populations' participation. Without this information, arts institutions are likely to find it difficult to design and implement effective strategies for reaching target populations.

Similarly, current and potential participants need information about arts organizations if they are to make informed choices. The types of information they will need vary depending on where they are in the decisionmaking process. Individuals not inclined to participate in the arts will need to be convinced that the arts organization and its programs have something to offer them. Those inclined to participate in the institution's programs but not currently doing so will need information on what the institution has to offer and when. Those already participating in an institution's programs need to understand why becoming more involved is of benefit to them.

In developing strategies for providing and gathering information, arts organizations need to consider not only what information they need or what message they want to convey, but also what methods of collecting and disseminating information work best. In other words, they must familiarize themselves with the most effective ways to collect information from potential and current participants, how the different types of participants gather information about leisure activity choices, and the kinds of messages most likely to resonate with each type.

This task of effectively collecting information about target populations and then disseminating information to those populations can be quite challenging. And what our survey results suggest is that many arts organizations do not give these issues sufficient attention. By and large, the institutions we surveyed were likely to rely on discussions among their staff as a primary means of gathering information about participants. It is unclear whether informal techniques such as this one are well-suited to collecting the kind of attitudinal and behavioral information about current and potential participants that we believe are key to developing effective engagement strategies. Similarly, although these organizations use a wide variety of techniques to disseminate information about their programs, no more than 40 percent of them rated these techniques as effective. We suspect that the problem here may not be the channels used to put information before the public per se but, rather, knowing when to use those channels and for which target groups.

Finally, although arts organizations will in all likelihood concentrate their engagement efforts on individuals considering participation or already participating in the arts, they need to be aware that the largest pool of potential participants most likely consists not of these individuals but of people not inclined to participate. The task of convincing this population is apt to be difficult, since it requires that arts institutions change these people's attitudes. While the long-run payoffs associated with increasing the participation of this population can be significant, investing resources in this purpose can entail significant opportunity costs for organizations with inadequate resources to begin with. Thus, organizations will need to strike a balance between targeting individuals at different points in the decisionmaking process.

NEED FOR AN INTEGRATIVE APPROACH

Participation-building efforts are likely to require considerable amounts of an organization's time and other resources—resources that otherwise could be used for arts programming and other artistic activities or for other institutional needs. It is therefore very important that an arts organization take an integrative approach to participation building; that is,

- Begin by considering how the organization's participation-building activities align with its core values and purpose by choosing participation goals that support its purpose.

- Identify clear target populations and base its tactics on good information about those groups.

- Understand what internal and external resources can be committed to building participation.

- Establish a process for feedback and self-evaluation.

Successful participation-building efforts require the commitment of an organization's key staff and operating units, its board, and its key funders. Such shared commitment must be based on the conviction that sustained audience development is critical to achieving the organization's mission. This requires an organization to articulate a clear set of participation goals that serve its basic mission and purpose and for which it can build consensus. Without this link, participation-building activities may be perceived as serving multiple and conflicting purposes or, even worse, as marginal to the organization's real work.

Once the participation goals have been chosen, the next step is to set out an operational plan for achieving these goals. Such a plan incorporates basic tactical decisions such as which target populations to choose, how to gather and analyze information about those populations, and what tactics to employ based on this knowledge.

The next step is to consider how to implement the operational plan—i.e., what resources are needed and how they will be obtained. The organization will have to take stock of its own internal assets (including staff, professional abilities, facilities, and equipment), and the alternative uses to which these assets might be applied. Indeed, an organization should consider how building participation can influence its entire operation, including its artistic programs and its ability to fulfill its institutional mission.

Since few organizations will have all the resources they need to implement their plans, they will have to carefully determine what resources might be available within the larger community. Collaborating with other institutions is one way to expand the resources an organization has at its disposal, but the effectiveness of collaboration depends on how much the goals of the parties to the collaboration complement each other.

Arts organizations must remember that no matter how carefully they align their engagement effort with their broader institutional mission, develop their operational plan, and assess their internal and external resources, it is very unlikely that the entire process will be straightforward or work exactly as planned. That is why it is essential that the final step of an integrative approach be to build a process for evaluation and feedback. This requires organizations to think carefully about what yardsticks they might use to gauge the success of their efforts and how to implement those yardsticks. Because success most likely cannot be measured exclusively in quantitative terms, organizations should also consider other, more qualitative measures with which to evaluate the success of their participation-building activities and whether those engagement activities serve their wider mission. Finally, arts organizations need to decide how to incorporate their assessments into their ongoing activities.

GUIDELINES FOR BUILDING PARTICIPATION

As should be clear, an arts organization's participation-building strategies must be tailored both to its target population and to its broader institutional context. Since both of these factors will vary across organizations, it is not surprising that we are not proposing one strategy or one set of best practices for all organizations. This does not mean, however, that there are no general guidelines that organizations should bear in mind as they develop and execute participation-building strategies. Indeed, the survey results reported in Appendices A and B demonstrate that there is a good deal of similarity in how organizations pursue participation building. The range of options that organizations may consider is large, but it is not boundless. In an effort to provide guidance for how to approach the task of participation building, we offer the following summarized list of guidelines grouped according to where they fit within the participation-building framework.

General Points:

1. Recognize that building participation is hard work and requires serious commitments of time and other resources.

2. Recognize that participation building is a team effort requiring continuous communication both inside the organization (with staff and board) and outside the organization (with community collaborators).

3. Know the organization and its capabilities, including its strengths and weaknesses.

4. Be aware that building participation is not a straightforward task and can involve developing different tactics for different target populations. Recognize that limited resources will often require tradeoffs among competing goals.

Setting Participation Goals

5. Set goals that are both realistic and consistent.

6. In identifying goals, look rigorously at the organization's purpose and at how building participation supports that purpose.

7. For all goals, be clear about what "increasing participation" means, what groups are to be the focus of the participation-building efforts, and how progress might be measured.

Choosing Target Populations

8. Determine what might motivate target groups to participate in the institution's programs, what the most important barriers to their participation are, and what the best techniques for addressing both these factors are.

9. Understand where the target population is in the decisionmaking process, since this is the key to developing effective tactics.

10. Do not ignore the population not inclined to participate. It may be harder to reach, but the reward for the effort could be significant.

11. Recognize that the choice of target population directly affects the resources needed to develop effective strategies, and that tradeoffs may well have to be made when choosing where to set priorities.

Tactics

12. Remember that to be effective, tactics must be targeted.

13. In choosing an operational plan, recognize that some factors can be controlled and some cannot. Focus your efforts on the former.

Information Strategies

14. Recognize that effective information strategies demand a two-way exchange of information: from the target population to the organization and from the organization to the target population.

15. Remember that to be effective, an information strategy must identify the target population, the most effective method for reaching that population, and the message that is to be conveyed.

Resources

16. Recognize that the institution is part of a community. Get to know that community and its organizations, including their strengths and weaknesses and how they complement the institution's.

17. Pursue collaborative relationships with other organizations with a clear understanding of what each party can bring to the collaboration and with a shared commitment to the same goals.

Evaluation and Feedback

18. Recognize that success in participation building is not simply a question of numbers. Consider how to evaluate your progress both quantitatively and qualitatively and how to gauge success even if it cannot be measured.

19. Since "getting it right" the first time is unlikely, be sure to evaluate progress and modify plans accordingly.

SURVEY RESULTS: ORGANIZATIONAL CHARACTERISTICS

As noted in Chapter One, we conducted a survey of arts organizations to collect systematic information about the characteristics of arts organizations and the specific things organizations do to build participation. This appendix and Appendix B describe the results of our survey of the actual participation-building activities of 102 arts institutions. This appendix illustrates the diversity of purpose, mission, resources, and environments of the organizations in our survey sample. As the data show, organizations with similar purposes tend to share characteristics: they emphasize similar mission elements, have similar levels of resources at their command, get their primary funding from similar sources, and enjoy similar types of community support. Institutions with different purposes contrast with each other in terms of many of these same characteristics. Appendix B shows how the various institutional similarities and differences are reflected in the goals and tactics of institutions seeking to build participation in their programs.

In reviewing these findings, it is important to bear in mind that they describe the organizations we interviewed and not the population of arts organizations as a whole. Indeed, because our sample came from populations of current and former grantees of the Wallace-Reader's Digest Funds and the Knight Foundation, there are several reasons to expect that our findings are not generalizable to all arts organizations. Both the Funds and the Knight Foundation have been particularly interested in building public participation in the arts, which means the organizations in our sample will be more concerned with increasing participation than would arts organizations chosen at random. Moreover, institutions were often chosen to be grantees because of their specific characteristics—the Funds' grants to visual arts institutions, for example, purposely focused on organizations with large budgets—or because they promised to employ specific tactics in their participation-building activities.

Our survey sample thus is not typical of arts organizations as a whole or even of organizations with similar purposes and missions. We nonetheless believe our findings are useful for highlighting the way a large number of organizations have expanded their audiences. As the data show, these organizations all take a similar approach to participation-building, but they also pursue a range of different goals and tactics in the process, many of which are related to their specific purposes and missions.

PURPOSE AND MISSION

As noted in Chapter Five, most organizations in our survey were able to clearly state their missions but were less explicit about their underlying purposes. All of the organizations articulated the specific goals of their various activities—such as increasing community involvement in their organization, fostering an appreciation of art among their participants, and training new artists—but most were less clear about their ultimate purpose. Using information provided by the Funds and the Knight Foundation, we were able to infer that the organizations we visited could be classified into three types according to purpose: those principally dedicated to supporting the canons of specific art forms (i.e., canon-focused), those principally dedicated to improving their communities using art as a vehicle (i.e., community-focused), and those principally dedicated to engaging individuals in the creative process and training new artists (i.e.,

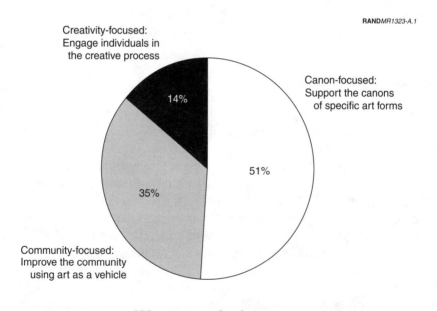

102 arts organizations

Figure A.1—Percentages of Three Different Types of Arts Organizations in Survey Sample

creativity-focused). Figure A.1 shows the percentage of the 102 arts organizations in our survey that fell within each of these three purpose-based classifications.

Mission Elements

During our site visits, we identified nine different mission elements that were salient to arts organizations:

- Fostering appreciation of the arts

- Increasing the public's exposure to the arts

- Improving the community using art as a vehicle

- Presenting and displaying new art (including performing art)

- Involving participants in the creative process (e.g., in creating a mural or putting on a production)

- Preserving and collecting existing works of art (including theater, dance, symphonies)

- Creating new art (e.g., commissioning new work)

- Training artists

- Funding artistic endeavors

We asked the organizations to report on the importance of these elements to their mission statements; Table A.1 reports their responses. As can be seen, the

Table A.1

How the Organizations Ranked Importance of Mission Elements

Mission Element	Overall Importance to Institution's Mission[a]	Percentage of Organizations Identifying Element as Primary
Foster appreciation	4.7	16
Expose people to art	4.7	28
Improve community	4.3	19
Present new art	4.1	20
Inspire creativity	3.5	20
Preserve existing art	3.5	13
Create new art	3.5	14
Train artists	2.8	12
Fund art	2.8	3

[a]Survey ratings: 1 = not at all; 2 = a little; 3 = a fair amount; 4 = much; 5 = very much.

organizations placed the most emphasis on fostering an appreciation of art and exposing people to the arts. These mission elements emphasize personal involvement with the arts. A number of other elements on the list have a similar emphasis on process and their effects: improving community, inspiring creativity, and training artists. Other mission elements focus on the art objects or performances themselves: making new and existing art available, preserving and collecting existing works of art, presenting or displaying new art, creating new art, and funding artistic endeavors.

Relationship Between Mission and Purpose

As the results in Table A.1 indicate, all of the organizations have several components to their missions, reflecting multiple goals not viewed as mutually exclusive. However, the priority placed on the mission elements differs with institutional purpose. Table A.2 shows how each of the three types of organizations in each class ranked the mission elements in terms of importance. Table A.3 shows the percentage of each class of organization that ranked each mission element as the most important to its mission.

Like the aggregate-level results in Table A.1, Table A.2's results indicate that all arts organizations in our sample considered changing individuals' relationship to art—particularly fostering appreciation and exposing people to art—to be critical to their mission. Community-focused and especially creativity-focused organizations placed much greater emphasis on involving participants directly in the creative process (e.g., inspiring creativity, training, and creating new art).

Table A.2

**How the Three Types of Organizations Ranked Importance
of Mission Elements**

Mission Element	Type of Organization		
	Canon-Focused	Community-Focused	Creativity-Focused
Foster appreciation	4.6	4.9	4.8
Expose people to art	4.7	4.7	4.3
Improve community	4.3	4.2	4.5
Present new art	4.1	4.2	3.8
Inspire creativity	3.1	3.8	4.4
Preserve existing art	4.2	2.7	2.5
Create new art	3.3	3.5	3.9
Train artists	2.6	2.8	4.4
Fund art	2.6	3.0	3.1

NOTE: Ratings are 1 = not at all; 2 = a little; 3 = a fair amount; 4 = much; 5 = very much.

Somewhat surprisingly, all three types appear to have placed considerable importance on improving communities through art. This finding suggests that organizations seeking to increase participation recognize the important role communities can play in this process.

As shown in Table A.3, canon-focused organizations placed their highest priority on activities associated with art presentation and collection, as is reflected in the proportion whose primary mission element relates to exposing people to art, preserving and collecting existing art, and presenting new art. In contrast, creativity-focused organizations placed a higher priority on the creative aspects of art, as is reflected in the importance assigned to inspiring creativity, training artists, and creating new art. Community-focused organizations lie somewhere between the canon- and creativity-focused institutions. Thus, in addition to concentrating on exposing more people to art and fostering an appreciation of art, they assign high priority to improving the community and presenting new art.

A somewhat surprising finding in Table A.3 is that community-focused organizations are no more likely to assign the highest priority to community improvement than are creativity-focused institutions. The explanation may be that institutions devoted to promoting individual creativity understand that getting participants involved in "doing" art requires a higher level of commitment than just getting them to appreciate the canon. To inspire such commitment, these organizations must become more deeply involved than canon-focused organizations in the community.

Table A.3

Percentage of Different Types of Organizations That Identified Each Mission Element as Primary

Mission Element	Type of Organization		
	Canon-Focused	Community-Focused	Creativity-Focused
Foster appreciation	15	19	7
Expose people to art	29	36	7
Improve community	10	28	29
Present new art	23	22	0
Inspire creativity	8	14	29
Preserve existing art	31	8	7
Create new art	12	14	21
Train artists	8	6	43
Fund art	6	0	7

One final point is noteworthy. Respondents were asked to identify the primary, or most important, of the mission elements. However, as can be seen by summing the percentage columns in the tables, the outcome was not one primary element per organization. The average number of primary elements identified totaled almost 1.5 elements per organization, which means almost half of the organizations in each category cited at least two primary elements. This suggests the difficulty many of these organizations faced in trying to identify the single most important aspect of their activities.

Discipline

One feature that may contribute to the difficulty the organizations had in assigning priorities to the various mission elements is their multidisciplinary nature. Although the vast majority of the organizations were able to identify one discipline as the *focus* of their programs (see Figure A.2), only 36 percent of them worked within a single discipline. Across our sample, organizations worked within one to six disciplines, with a median of three.[1] This average, however, differed by predominant discipline, as shown in Figure A.3.

On average, theater and literary organizations worked in fewer disciplines than did music and dance organizations, with visual arts organizations falling in be-

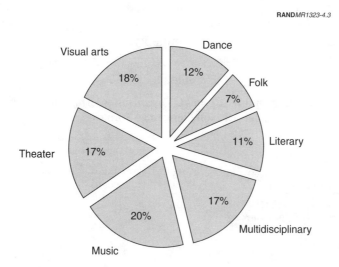

RAND*MR1323-4.3*

Figure A.2—Predominant Disciplines Reported by Organizations

---

[1]The median represents the midpoint of the distribution. Half the organizations lie above the median value and half below.

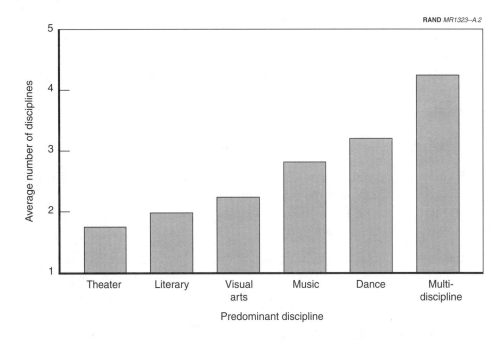

Figure A.3—Multidisciplinary Nature of the Organizations

tween. In addition, about 23 percent of these organizations were unable to identify a predominant discipline. Many of them focus on presenting works in a variety of disciplines or specialize in the folk arts, which by their nature include elements of several disciplines. For these multidisciplinary organizations, the average number of disciplines was 4.3.[2]

As a general proposition, the more disciplines an organization works within, the more difficulty it will have developing coherent engagement strategies and tactics and allocating resources accordingly. As one of our respondents described it, organizations involved in multiple disciplines face the challenge of "being all things to all people."

Discipline and Purpose

Our survey results show that canon-focused organizations worked with fewer disciplines than did community- or creativity-focused organizations. As Figure A.4 shows, canon-focused organizations were much less likely to describe themselves as multidisciplinary. Instead, most of them concentrate on visual

---

[2]The multidisciplinary organizations represent organizations unable to choose a predominant discipline.

arts, music, and literary arts. Community-focused organizations were more often multidisciplinary or emphasized theater. Creativity-focused organizations were concentrated in multiple disciplines, visual arts, music, and dance. No creativity-focused organizations concentrated on folk or literary arts.[3]

INTERNAL RESOURCES

Organizations have a variety of personnel and operational needs, as well as the need to adapt to changes in both their internal circumstances and the external environment (Shortell and Kaluzny, 1994). The ways organizations manifest these needs, however, and the internal and external resources they have to address them, vary with such structural features of the organization as age, budgets, sources of revenues, and boards.

As the data in this section show, canon-focused organizations tend to be older and have much larger budgets than the other two types of organizations.

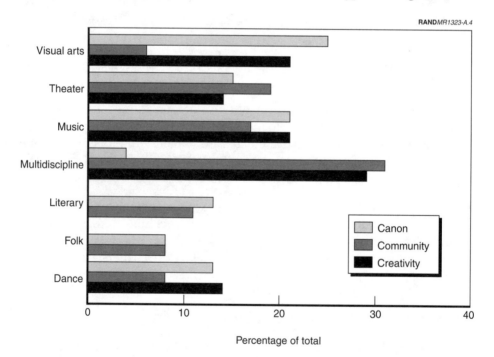

RAND*MR1323-A.4*

Percentage of total

Figure A.4—Primary Disciplines of the Different Types of Organizations

---

[3]Once again, it is important to remember that these results are based on the sample of institutions we interviewed, not all arts organizations. Since both the Funds and the Knight Foundation choose grantees with specific purposes in mind, one cannot assume that these distributions are representative of arts institutions in general.

Community-focused organizations are the youngest in our survey group. They also have the smallest budgets and are less visible and more likely to depend on foundations and government, rather than individual philanthropy, for their support. Creativity-focused organizations fall between these two extremes. They typically are younger and considerably less well-funded than canon-focused organizations but are older and better-funded than community-focused organizations.

Age

The needs of organizations change over their life cycles. As we heard at several of our site visits, young organizations are often dominated by the vision, energy, and personality of their founder. As they age, a critical test of resiliency is whether they can develop the staffing and support infrastructures needed to sustain themselves once the founder is no longer the dominant figure. Indeed, one of the central needs of all organizations is adapting to change, both internal and external. Organizations that not only survive but prosper in a changing environment are likely to achieve increasing visibility and legitimacy within their communities. Thus, organizations have different needs and access to resources at different stages of their development.

Figure A.5 compares the median age of the organizations we surveyed. About half had been in existence for 30 years. In general, there was little variation

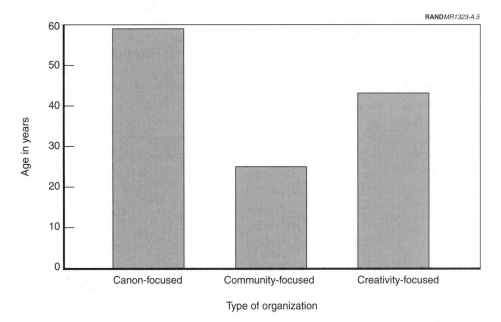

Figure A.5—Average Age of Different Types of Organizations

around this median, since about 65 percent of all the organizations were be-tween 15 and 50 years old. About 15 percent were less than 15 years old, and about 20 percent were over 75 years old.

This pattern varied somewhat for the three different types of organizations. Canon-focused organizations had a median age of almost 60 years and thus were older than their community- and creativity-focused counterparts, whose medians were 25 and 43 years, respectively. One factor that may have con-tributed to these age differences was the concentration of visual arts institu-tions in the canon- and creativity-focused categories. Over 50 percent of the visual arts organizations in our sample had been in existence for over 85 years, and less than 33 percent for under 50 years. To the extent that an organization's specific needs and access to resources vary by age, we might expect these fac-tors to vary by organizational purpose.

Budgets

Just as the average age of the institutions differed, so too did the overall size of their budgets.[4] About 20 percent of the organizations had total budgets of $750,000 or less; another 20 percent had budgets of over $10 million. Overall, the median budget was $3.75 million and the average was close to $20 million. This substantial difference between the median and the average arises because while the budgets of most of the organizations were clustered around $3 million to $4 million, a few very large organizations had very large budgets.

We also found that as had been true for age, budget size varied with primary purpose. With an average budget of almost $35 million, canon-focused organi-zations had about four times more to spend than did creativity-focused organi-zations ($8.7 million) and over 15 times more than did community-focused or-ganizations ($2.5 million). Clearly the scale of operation, the resources avail-able, and in all likelihood the complexity of these organizations differ by pre-dominant purpose. Community-focused organizations are much younger and much smaller than the canon-focused organizations, and creativity-focused or-ganizations fall between these two extremes.

Sources of Revenue

Table A.4 displays a final structural difference among the organizations we in-terviewed: their sources of revenue. Five major funding sources are listed: earned income (receipts from ticket and other sales and tuition), grants from

---

[4]About one-third of the organizations reported budget totals for earlier years. We adjusted these budgets to 1999 by using an annual adjustment factor of 3 percent per year.

Table A.4

Breakdown of Revenue Sources for the Three Types of Organizations
(percentage of revenue by source)

Source of Revenue	Canon-Focused	Community-Focused	Creativity-Focused	All
Earned income	40	36	39	39
Receipts	39	33	12	34
Tuition	1	3	27	5
Grants	22	42	30	30
Foundations	13	24	11	17
Government	9	18	19	13
Donations	25	15	19	20
Corporate	5	5	7	5
Individual	12	6	6	9
Other	8	4	6	6
Endowment income	8	1	3	5
Other	5	6	9	6

foundations and government, donations (from corporations, individuals, and fundraising events), endowment income, and income from all other sources. Overall, the organizations received a higher share of their revenues from earnings—about 40 percent of the total—than from any other source, and within the earnings category, receipts from tickets and other sales outpaced tuition payments by close to 7 to 1. Grant income constituted the second largest source of income—about 33 percent of the total; donations represented about 20 percent, and the last two sources—endowment income and other income—each constituted less than 10 percent.

This general pattern, however, differs sharply for the three types of organizations. Although the overall share of revenue coming from earnings does not in itself differ dramatically among the three types, the sources of the earnings do. Canon-focused organizations received almost all of their earned income from ticket and other sales. Creativity-focused organizations, in contrast, received more than 66 percent of their earnings from tuition payments. Canon-focused organizations also received a larger share of their revenues from donations, especially from individuals, and were the only organizations that received significant income from endowments. Community-focused organizations received more than 40 percent of their total income from grants—and almost 25 percent of this was from foundations.

In comparing these results, it is important to bear in mind that these percentages are calculated on very different total revenue bases. The average community-focused organization, for example, has a total revenue base of about

$2.5 million, whereas the average canon-focused organization has a budget 15 times that size. Thus, both the sources of revenue and the amount of money received from those sources vary across organizations. Such differences, of course, translate into large differences in the resources these organizations have.

Several reasons may be causing these differences, including local funding circumstances, institutional traditions, board and staff preferences, and disciplinary practices, all of which are beyond the scope of this report. However, as our discussion of mission elements makes clear, both the types of activities that organizations sponsor and the priorities assigned to these activities differ by organizational purpose. These differences have implications for organizational funding. This point may be clearest as regards earned income—the largest source of revenue for all three types of organizations. Canon-focused organizations place the highest priority on presenting art and receive the highest fraction of their income from ticket and related sales. Creativity-focused organizations are much more involved in training artists and rely much more heavily on tuition payments than on admissions receipts for their earned income.

It is also interesting to note that these differences in revenue sources are correlated with an organization's age. Community-focused organizations, which are considerably more likely to rely on grants from foundations, are younger and smaller than the other two types of organizations. Canon-focused organizations, which receive about twice as much of their total budgets from individual donations, are older and larger than the other types of organizations. They are also the only type to receive any substantial income from endowments—a characteristic of well-established and well-supported institutions.

These comparisons also suggest that the broader needs of arts organizations are likely to differ with purpose and activities. Because organizations need to be sensitive to how their engagement strategies (and other policies) affect their principal funders and because these funding sources differ, engagement strategies may be influenced by these differences. Similarly, the different budgets and ages of the organizations suggest that they may face different organizational issues. Older organizations with a long history in their communities, for example, have well-established reputations and an extensive series of community contacts. This provides them with a stamp of approval from some groups, such as the media and those who are already supporters of the arts, but it may have a different effect on other constituents, such as people unfamiliar with the arts or who think the institution serves only elite audiences and thus not them. Younger organizations, in contrast, may have less visibility and thus need to determine what message they want to convey about their organization, to which groups, and in what ways. How organizations deal with these issues may affect how they are perceived not only by the wider community but also by their target populations, their funders, other community institutions, and even their own staffs.

Boards

All of the organizations we interviewed had governing or advisory boards. Board members are traditionally chosen for the special skills that they can bring to an organization, which typically include fundraising, marketing, financial expertise, business management, legal expertise, property management, artistic expertise, media contact, and community development. The organizations we interviewed are no exception to this pattern. Fundraising, financial expertise, business management, legal expertise, and community development skills were found in over 90 percent of the boards of these organizations, and artistic expertise and marketing skills were present in over 80 percent.

Table A.5 presents the average number of board members for each type of organization and the percentage of each type of organization having board members representative of its target populations—a tactic many of the surveyed organizations used to help them understand and reach out to the communities they want to serve. The boards ranged from 6 to 90 members, with an average of about 30. The boards of canon-focused organizations were about half again as large as those of the other two types of organizations. About half of these boards included representatives of target populations—a pattern more characteristic of community-focused than of canon- or creativity-focused organizations.

Finally, Table A.6 compares the functions served by the boards in these organizations.[5] The specific functions examined here include strategic planning, plan-

Table A.5

Average Size of Boards and Inclusion of Target Population on Boards for the Three Types of Organizations

Type	Average Size	Percentage of Boards Including Members of Target Group
Canon-focused	34	44
Community-focused	22	62
Creativity-focused	21	43
All	28	50

---

[5]In addition to their formal advisory boards, about half of these organizations (57 percent) convene special community advisory groups to assist them in community outreach efforts.

Table A.6

Functions of the Boards of the Three Types of Organizations

Type	Strategic Planning	Arts Programming	Fundraising	Marketing	Community Contact
Canon-focused	4.2	1.9	4.3	2.8	3.7
Community-focused	4.1	2.1	4.3	3.3	3.5
Creativity-focused	4.2	2.7	4.2	3.2	4.0
All	4.2	2.1	4.3	3.0	3.7

NOTE: Survey asked whether board serves this function. 1 = never; 2 = rarely; 3 = sometimes; 4 = frequently.

ning of arts programs, fundraising, marketing, and community outreach. Two of these roles—fundraising and strategic planning—clearly predominate: the vast majority of the boards filled these roles either "frequently" or "almost always." Boards are also often used as a vehicle for establishing contacts or networking within the community, but are used less frequently to market an institution's activities and are generally not used at all to help plan artistic offerings. There is little variation in the ways the three types of organizations use their boards. However, creativity-focused organizations and to some extent community-focused organizations are more inclined than are canon-focused organizations to involve their boards in marketing and planning activities.

EXTERNAL RESOURCES

To supplement their internal resources, organizations often form collaborations with outside groups or individuals to gain needed skills or services. In the survey, we asked organizations about two different types of such collaborations: those with artists and those with community groups.

Almost all of the organizations involved artists in some aspect of their activities. Our survey asked specifically about the degree to which organizations sponsor artists in residence, include artists in outreach activities, work with artists in planning artistic programs, and employ artists to teach classes or hold workshops. Figure A.6 shows the results. About 75 percent of these organizations used artists "frequently" or "almost always" to teach classes and hold workshops and to help the organization reach out to the community. Artists were provided residencies somewhat less frequently (about 60 percent of the time) and were used "frequently" to help plan programs by less than 50 percent of the organizations.

Although all three types of arts organizations assign essentially the same priorities to these uses, the frequency of usage varies systematically according to the organization's principal purpose (see Table A.7). Creativity-focused organiza-

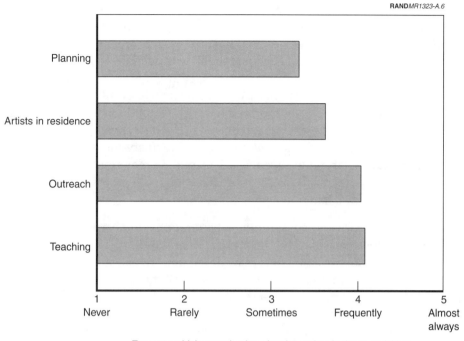

Extent to which organizations involve artists in these activities

Figure A.6—Use of Artists in Building Participation

Table A.7

Use of Artists by the Three Types of Organizations

Type	Teaching	Outreach	Artist in Residence	Planning
Canon-focused	3.8	3.8	3.4	3.2
Community-focused	4.2	4.1	3.7	3.3
Creativity-focused	4.6	4.6	4.3	4.1

NOTE: 1 = almost never; 2 = rarely; 3 = sometimes; 4 = almost always.

tions use artists more frequently than the other organizations in each of the
four ways—indeed, they uniformly use artists "frequently" or "almost always"
in all four ways. Canon-focused organizations use artists less than the other two
types of organizations do. This pattern is consistent with the different importance these three types of organizations attach to involving participants in the
creative process. However, it also indicates the ways in which an organization's
purpose can affect not only its participation-building activities but also its
broader interactions with the community.

We also asked survey respondents about the frequency with which they interact with such community groups as schools, libraries, other cultural organizations, health and social service agencies, and businesses (see Table A.8). Virtually all respondents reported high levels of interaction with schools—perhaps a reflection of their commitment to influencing the next generation to become engaged in the arts. The organizations also reported high levels of interaction with other cultural organizations, but formed fewer collaborations with businesses, health and social service agencies, and libraries. The only substantial difference in these patterns was the greater involvement of creativity-focused institutions with health and social service agencies. This finding may reflect the fact that creativity-focused organizations are more likely than the others to become involved with their participants at a personal level.

Arts organizations turn to community collaborations for a variety of reasons. Table A.9 lists these reasons and the average importance the respondents gave to each one. No one reason emerges as dominant; indeed, the organizations cited only two for which they rely on outside collaborators "relatively frequently": to provide entrée into communities and to help promote their activities. More typically, they relied on community resources from "sometimes" to "rarely." When they did, the reason was more likely to be to help publicize activities or for general support—i.e., to share mailing lists and performance spaces or provide political support and legitimacy. Only rarely did they seek advice or technical assistance from outside groups or share materials or operations with them.

These general patterns, however, do not hold equally for all three types of arts organizations. Creativity-focused organizations are much more likely than the other two types to use community collaborators for a broad range of purposes. Indeed, unlike their counterparts, they frequently seek a wide variety of benefits.

Table A.8

Frequency of Collaboration with Community Groups for the Three Types of Organizations

Community Group	Canon-Focused	Community-Focused	Creativity-Focused	All
Schools	4.5	4.3	4.4	4.4
Other cultural organizations	4.0	4.1	4.3	4.1
Business	3.3	3.3	3.0	3.3
Health and social services	2.6	3.1	3.7	2.9
Libraries	2.8	2.5	2.7	2.6

NOTE: 1 = almost never; 2 = rarely; 3 = sometimes; 4 = almost always.

Table A.9

Reasons for Collaborating with Community Groups

Reason	All Respondents
Entrée to community	3.5
Promote activities	3.5
Share mailing lists	2.9
Structure events	2.9
Share performance space	2.7
Provide legitimacy	2.7
Provide political support	2.7
Access to artists	2.5
Provide technical assistance	2.5
Advise on programming	2.5
Share funds/staff, equipment	2.0
Share office space	1.6

NOTE: Survey asked whether collaborator serves this function. 1 = never; 2 = rarely; 3 = sometimes; 4 = frequently.

ENVIRONMENT

The focus so far has been on the characteristics of arts organizations themselves and the nature of their interactions with artists and community groups. These are central aspects of an institution's context, but they do not fully describe the environment in which an arts organization operates and to which it must adapt. An institution's local environment consists of a much wider range of organizations, including funders, arts and other cultural institutions, local governments, the media, and community-based organizations. The institutions we interviewed included both those well established in their communities and those relatively new and still seeking public visibility. How arts organizations are viewed by the broader community and how much support they receive from the community are important factors in their performance and success.

To gain a better understanding of the differing environments for the arts, we asked institutional leaders to evaluate the degree of support provided to the arts by various community organizations (see Table A.10). As might be expected, the support from these sources varied considerably. The most supportive institutions were those already having connections with the arts, such as foundations and other arts funders, leading cultural institutions, and community-based arts organizations. Local government and the media were less supportive, and community-based non-arts organizations were the least.

In general, the differences in the degree of support across the three different types of arts organizations were not large, but they were suggestive. Local gov-

Table A.10

Support for the Arts from Different Community Organizations

Community Organization	Type of Organization			
	Canon-Focused	Community-Focused	Creativity-Focused	All
Local foundations, funders	4.2	3.9	3.7	4.0
Leading cultural institutions	4.0	3.6	3.9	3.9
Local government	2.3	3.3	3.1	3.1
Local press	3.4	3.3	2.3	3.3
Community-based arts organizations	3.7	3.8	3.3	3.8
Community-based non-arts organizations	2.4	2.4	2.6	2.4

NOTE: Survey asked about extent of support. 1 = not at all; 2 = a little; 3 = a fair amount; 4 = much; 5 = very much.

ernments appear to be somewhat more involved in organizations more focused on community development. In contrast, local foundations and funders, leading cultural institutions, and the press were more involved in the activities of canon-focused organizations. Although we did not ask organizations for the reasons behind their rankings, it is clear that the age and size of canon-focused organizations bring them more public recognition than the other two types of organizations achieve. Do the older, larger, and wealthier institutions receive more support because they are more established? Or do they receive more support because they can afford the time and resources to establish and maintain connections with these other community institutions? Perhaps the answer is both.

SURVEY RESULTS: PARTICIPATION-BUILDING ACTIVITIES

This appendix examines the approaches organizations use to build participation. Following the sequence of steps involved in the participation-building process, we begin by looking at the goals of the participation-building efforts, including how organizations define increasing participation and how increasing participation relates to organizational purpose and mission. We then turn to how institutions select target populations and go about collecting information about current and potential participants. This information-gathering process identifies both the reasons why individuals may be attracted to the arts and the various obstacles that might stand in the way of their participation. Using that knowledge, organizations set out to design tactics to help people overcome the obstacles; they then allocate the resources needed to implement those tactics.

In the following discussion, we report on how the institutions we surveyed approached each of these tasks. We first look at these participation-building activities for all organizations, then compare differences across organizations with similar primary purposes.

SETTING GOALS

Given that almost all of the organizations we interviewed noted that resource constraints (in terms of dollars, staff, and time) affected their participation activities, we expected that they might limit their participation-building efforts to one or at most two of the three goals for participation: broadening participation, diversifying it, and deepening it. However, approximately half of the organizations responded "very much" when asked how much they focused on each of these goals. This pattern also held when the survey results were tabulated by type of organization—i.e., those focused principally on the canons of specific art forms, those focused principally on improving their communities using art as a vehicle, and those focused principally on engaging individuals in the creative process and training new artists (see Table B.1).

Table B.1

**Relative Emphasis on Participation Goals Reported by the
Three Types of Organizations**

Participation-Building Goal	Type of Organization		
	Canon-Focused	Community-Focused	Creativity-Focused
Broaden	4.3	4.4	4.1
Diversify	4.3	4.4	4.6
Deepen	4.1	4.3	4.4

NOTE: Survey asked about extent to which organization focuses on this goal. 1 = not at all; 2 = little; 3 = fair amount; 4 = much; 5 = very much.

This pattern contrasts sharply with what the Funds' staff told us about the participation goals of their grantees, however. According to the Funds, there are clear and often sharp differences in the priorities the different types of organizations place on the three participation goals (see Table B.2). The results in this case show that canon-focused organizations are much more likely than the other two types of organizations to stress both broadening and diversifying their audience. The vast majority of creativity-focused organizations (86 percent) gave the greatest effort to deepening participation. Community-focused organizations fall between these two extremes: Half of them concentrated on deepening involvement, about a third on broadening participation, and the rest on diversifying participation.

We are not sure what accounts for this discrepancy. It may be that self-reports do not reflect the priorities organizations actually attach to the different goals, or that organizations do not differentiate clearly between these goals, considering them all part of participation building. It may also be that the organizations are simply unwilling to assign a higher priority to one goal because they are aware that the Funds values each goal equally.

Table B.2

**Funds' Evaluation of Emphasis Organizations Give to
Participation Goals
(in percentage)**

Participation-Building Goal	Type of Organization		
	Canon-Focused	Community-Focused	Creativity-Focused
Broaden	44	31	7
Diversify	40	19	7
Deepen	16	50	86

DEFINING SERVICE COMMUNITIES

In addition to deciding what form of increasing participation they seek, organizations must identify whom they want to target. This process typically requires two steps: defining their service communities and identifying the specific groups within those communities that will be the target of their participation efforts.

Table B.3 shows how the institutions surveyed defined their service areas. Almost 75 percent defined their market areas geographically—perhaps not terribly surprising since it is much easier to identify and serve participants located close to the institution. Indeed, some of the institutions (such as those in rural areas or that define their service community as an entire state or region) stressed the difficulties they face in attempting to serve such broad geographic areas.

Table B.3

Definition of Service Areas by the Three Types of Organizations

Definition	Type of Organization			
	Canon-Focused	Community-Focused	Creativity-Focused	All
Geographic	3.8	4.1	4.0	4.0
Demographic	3.3	4.1	3.7	3.7
Behavior	3.5	3.4	3.4	3.4

NOTE: Survey asked about extent to which organization defines service areas in this way. 1 = not at all; 2 = little; 3 = fair amount; 4 = much; 5 = very much.

IDENTIFYING TARGET GROUPS

However an arts organization defines its service area, it still needs to determine which groups within that area it wants to target for its outreach efforts. As the participation model suggests, the more closely an organization can target its outreach efforts, the more successful (and efficient) its outreach efforts are likely to be. There are several different criteria organizations might use in selecting their target populations. They might, for example, select populations currently underserved or that are rapidly growing. Or they might base their choice on the nature of their current activities and how closely they align with different groups. Although we did not ask respondents how they identified the interests of their target groups, we did ask them *whether* they targeted their participation-building efforts and, if so, how they defined those target groups.

Only 84 percent of the organizations claimed they had identified a target population when directly asked that question. However, a thorough review of the
survey instruments suggested that almost all of the respondents (93 percent)
did in fact target their outreach efforts in some way. One reason for this apparent discrepancy may be that almost 20 percent of the respondents reported that
their target populations varied depending on the performance or exhibit being
presented. Almost 50 percent of these organizations relied exclusively on an
event-specific targeting strategy.

Among those organizations that identified target populations, some identified a
single group, some two groups, and others three or more (see Figure B.1). When
asked how they identified target groups, almost 75 percent responded that they
identified them demographically—that is, they defined their target populations
in terms of specific age or ethnic groups (see Table B.4). Twenty-eight percent
of the institutions identified their target populations geographically—for example, the residents of the state or of a particular neighborhood—and 28 percent defined their target populations in terms of interest in a specific art form.
Finally, 20 percent varied their targeting strategy with the type of program they
were sponsoring.

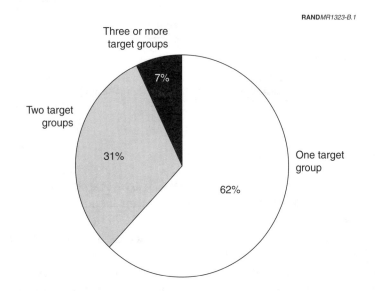

Figure B.1—Proportion of Organizations with One or More Target Groups

Table B.4

Organizations' Definitions of Their Target Population

Strategy	Percentage of Target Population[a]
Demographic	73
Age	43
Ethnicity	54
Income	14
Behavioral	28
Geographic	28
Varies with program	20
Other	3

[a]Since many organizations identify more than one target audience, the figures here sum to more than 100 percent. Also, 7 percent of the organizations reported they did not have a target group.

Table B.5 compares the targeting strategies of the three different types of institutions. By and large, there does not appear to be much difference across the three types. All three are most likely to define their target groups demographically and about equally likely to use one of the three other targeting strategies. The greater frequency with which community-focused organizations use all three of the approaches seems more likely to stem from the fact that these organizations average somewhat more (1.6) target populations than the canon- (1.2) or creativity-focused (1.3) organizations.

Although we did not specifically ask the organizations about the predisposition of their target groups, it is interesting that so few defined these groups in terms of behavior.

Table B.5

Definition of Target Populations by the Three Types of Organizations (in percentage)

	Type of Organization		
Definition	Canon-Focused	Community-Focused	Creativity-Focused
Geographic	23	31	21
Demographic	54	83	71
Behavior	19	28	21
Program-specific	19	19	14

GATHERING INFORMATION

Having identified its target populations, an organization needs to gather information about those populations in order to design strategies to influence their participation behavior. As noted in Chapter Three, which discusses the participation model, individuals fall along a continuum from those not interested in the arts to those truly committed to the arts. This distinction is important, because the types of barriers that organizations face in their efforts to increase participation will differ for different groups of individuals.

To gain a better understanding of the organizations' knowledge of their participants, we asked them how much they know about current participants and target populations, how they obtained this information, and what they viewed as the major motivations for and barriers to increasing participation for each of these groups.

How Much Do They Know?

As might be expected, the organizations knew considerably more about their current participants than their target populations (see Table B.6). Although almost two-thirds of them knew "very much" or "much" about their current participants, only about one-third knew an equivalent amount about their target population. Conversely, close to one-quarter knew little or nothing at all about their target populations, whereas less than 5 percent knew little or nothing about current participants. The most likely reason for this difference is that it is much easier to get information about current participants than about target populations. Contact with current participants is typically direct and often repeated. Most target groups are chosen specifically *because* they are not currently involved with the institution.

Table B.6

Assessments of Levels of Knowledge of Current Participants and
Target Populations by the Three Types of Organizations

	Type of Organization		
Group	Canon-Focused	Community-Focused	Creativity-Focused
Current participants	3.8	3.7	4.2
Target population	3.2	3.2	3.5

NOTE: Survey asked about extent to which organization is knowledgeable about this group. 1 = not at all; 2 = little; 3 = fair amount; 4 = much; 5 = very much.

All three types of organizations knew more about their current participants than about their target populations. However, creativity-focused organizations knew more about both groups than did canon- and community-focused organizations. This difference is consistent with the level of involvement required by creativity-focused institutions and the greater involvement they tend to have with their communities—a point demonstrated previously.

How Do Organizations Gather Information?

We also asked the organizations about their use of several informal and formal techniques to gather information. The informal techniques were discussions with staff, advisory committees, and community members; the formal techniques were surveys, focus groups, and other traditional marketing means. Figure B.2 compares the frequency with which these techniques were used for current participants and target populations.

The organizations were much more likely to use informal than formal techniques to collect information. Each of the three informal methods was used more frequently than any of the formal methods. Although less systematic, these informal methods are undoubtedly less costly than the formal methods.

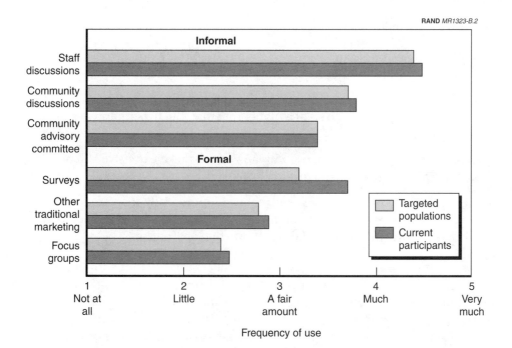

Figure B.2—Use of Informal and Formal Techniques for Gathering Information on Participation

In addition, the organizations may feel more comfortable using informal rather than formal methods because they are more familiar with the former.

Staff discussions were the most frequently used way to obtain information about participants and were also likely to be the least expensive in terms of dollars and staff time. Despite its cost advantage, however, this technique may introduce a selectivity problem in that staff discussions will be directly influenced by staff impressions of and interactions with individuals who may or may not be typical of the wider populations they are thought to represent.

Among the formal methods, surveys were used most frequently; however, they were used considerably more often to gather information about current participants than about target populations. This difference may reflect the fact that it is easier and less costly to identify and survey a sample of people already in contact with the organization than a sample of the population the organization is trying to reach.

Figure B.3 shows how information-gathering techniques varied by type of organization. To clarify the patterns here, we report the results only for current participants. The ways in which the organizations gather information about target populations were essentially the same as those for current participants except that each technique was used at a somewhat lower level.

There are several patterns worthy of note here:

- All three types of organizations rely more frequently on staff discussions than on any other technique.

- Creativity-focused organizations consistently rely more on informal than formal techniques and do so at a higher rate than the two other types of organizations.

- Canon- and community-focused organizations make extensive use of surveys to find out about their current participants.

- Canon-focused organizations are somewhat more likely than community-focused organizations and much more likely than creativity-focused organizations to use the other traditional marketing approaches.

The fact that organizations vary in how they collect information about participants reflects their different characteristics. Creativity-focused organizations take a more hands-on approach to participants than do canon- or community-focused organizations. Thus, they may well have more direct and detailed knowledge of their participants than do the other organizations. Canon-focused organizations, however, often have the resources to employ formal surveys and other traditional marketing techniques.

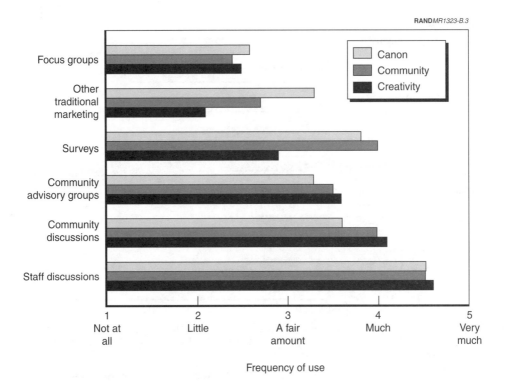

RAND*MR1323-B.3*

Figure B.3—Techniques Used by the Three Types of Organizations to Gather Information About Current Participants

What Do the Organizations Know About Motivations?

Finally, we asked the organizations what they knew about their participants and target populations. We first examine their understanding of the motivations of their current participants;[1] we then look at their responses to questions about the major barriers to increasing the participation of both current participants and target populations.

Each organization was asked, How many of your participants are involved in your organization's activities for these reasons? and provided nine reasons to rank on a scale of 1 to 5. Over half of the organizations cited five primary reasons that motivated either a "very large" or a "large" number of their current participants (see Figure B.4).

_____

[1]It is important to note that the motivations for and obstacles to participation discussed in this and the subsequent section are based on the responses of organizations, not individuals.

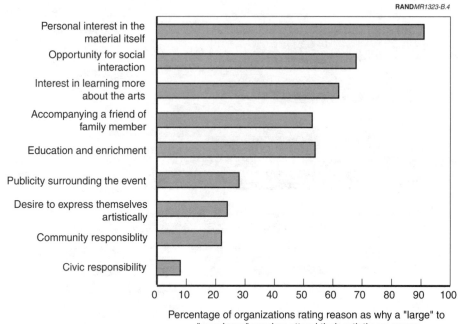

Figure B.4—Reasons Organizations Identified for Why People Participate in the Arts

They ranked the following reasons as the most important:

- **Personal interest in the material itself**. Over 90 percent said that either a "very large" or a "large" number of their participants were attracted to their programs because of their intrinsic interest in the material being presented. This finding seems to underscore our behavioral model's assertion that current participants in the arts are already interested in and predisposed toward the arts.

- **Opportunity for social interaction**. Approximately 70 percent said that a "very large" or a "large" number of their participants were motivated by the opportunity that participation provided to enjoy the company of others.

- **Interest in learning more about the arts**. Over 60 percent reported that at least a large number of their participants were attracted by their desire to learn more about the arts. This response, which is related to the personal interest motivation described above, underscores the notion that arts participants not only find the material interesting but want to know more about it.

- **Accompanying a friend or family member**. Almost 55 percent said that a "large" to a "very large" number of individuals participated because of their ties to someone else who had made the decision to participate.

- **Education and enrichment**. About 55 percent reported that a "very large" or "large" number of those who participated in their activities did so because they wanted to expose their family members to the arts. Presumably because the arts provide an enriching experience for them, they wanted to provide that experience to others. Note that although this motivation is related to accompanying a friend or family member, there is an important distinction. In the former case, the decision to participate is made by the friend or family member who invited the participant; in the latter case, the participant makes the decision.

Although these five reasons stand out, they were not the only reasons cited as motivating participants. About 25 percent of the organizations reported that a "very large" or "large" number of their participants were attracted by the "desire to express themselves artistically" or by the publicity surrounding their programs. Civic and community responsibilities were cited less frequently as reasons for participation.

Table B.7 shows how the responses to these motivation questions varied by type of organization. Although there are more similarities than differences evident in this table, three points are noteworthy:

- All three types of organizations reported that the foremost motivation of their participants is personal interest in the artistic material itself.

- Creativity-focused organizations were much more likely than their counterparts to report that their participants are motivated by a desire to express themselves artistically and to learn about the art form.

Table B.7

Ratings of Participants' Motivations by the Three Types of Organizations

| Motivations | Type of Organization | | |
	Canon-Focused	Community-Focused	Creativity-Focused
Personal interest	4.5	4.5	4.7
Social experience	3.9	3.9	3.6
Learn about art	3.8	3.6	4.4
Invited by family/friends	3.6	3.8	3.6
Education and enrichment	3.5	3.5	3.8
Publicity	3.0	3.2	2.4
Express self	2.6	2.8	4.1
Community	2.3	2.9	2.9
Civic duty	2.2	2.2	2.4

NOTE: Survey asked about the number of participants motivated by these factors. 1 = almost none; 2 = a small number; 3 = a fair number; 4 = a large number; 5 = a very large number.

- Compared to their counterparts, creativity-focused organizations were much less likely to report that their participants were motivated to participate as a result of the publicity surrounding the organization and its activities.

What Do the Organizations Know About Barriers to Participation?

We asked the organizations we interviewed about the potential importance of 15 separate barriers to individuals increasing their participation. In presenting the results, we have grouped these barriers into four general categories. Chapter Three discusses three of them: perceptual, practical, and experience-based barriers. We included a fourth—personal circumstances—which is often mentioned in the literature on participation. This category includes lack of leisure time and preference for other leisure activities.

Table B.8 provides the results. The higher the number shown, the stronger the barrier it poses to current nonparticipants, according to the respondents. The barriers are defined as follows:

- **Perceptual barriers:** (1) the nature of the art or art form does not appeal; (2) it is hard to connect with the meaning or message of the work; (3) would feel uncomfortable; (4) perceptions of elitism associated with the art form or organization.

- **Personal circumstances:** (1) difficult to make time; (2) rather spend leisure time in other ways; (3) cannot find anyone to go with; (4) friends or family would not understand interest.

- **Practical barriers:** (1) childcare problems; (2) organization is not accessible; (3) not sure what the organization does; (4) hours of operation are inconvenient; (5) location is not safe; (6) costs too much.

- **Prior experiences:** The individuals have not enjoyed their prior experience with the particular art form.

In discussing the results of Table B.8, we compare the findings first for current participants and then for target populations. We also report the average scores for each category of reasons.[2] The two most important obstacles to increasing participation that organizations identified both for current participants and for target populations are not related to participants' prior knowledge of, attitudes toward, or experience with the arts, but rather to their personal circumstances.

---

[2]Once again, it is important to note that these results are based on the responses of organizations, not individuals.

Table B.8

Organizations' Assessments of Barriers to Participation

Barrier	Current Participants	Target Population	Difference
Perceptual			
No appeal	2.11	2.94	0.83
Hard to connect	1.93	2.66	0.73
Uncomfortable	1.78	3.08	1.30
Elitist	1.74	2.69	0.95
Subtotal average	1.88	2.84	0.95
Personal circumstances			
Not enough time	3.09	3.46	0.37
Other leisure activities	2.65	3.52	0.87
No one to go with	1.75	2.36	0.61
Wouldn't understand interest	1.39	1.93	0.54
Subtotal average	2.22	2.82	0.60
Practical			
Childcare problems	2.44	2.88	0.44
Inaccessibility	2.16	2.85	0.69
Not sure what organization does	2.00	3.13	1.13
Hours inconvenient	1.64	1.81	0.17
Location unsafe	1.70	2.09	0.39
Costs too much	1.80	2.48	0.68
Subtotal average	1.96	2.54	0.58
Prior experience	1.66	2.15	0.49

NOTE: Survey asked about importance of barrier. 1 = not at all; 2 = little; 3 = fair amount; 4 = much; 5 = very much.

Specifically, the organizations reported that both current and potential participants are very busy and cannot find the time to participate in the arts as much as they might like. Moreover, the arts must compete with a host of other potential leisure activities for participants' time.

It is interesting to note that these two items are perceived as more of a barrier to target populations than to current participants—despite the fact that there is no reason to assume a priori that current participants have more free time than target populations do. Indeed, the fact that competing leisure time activities are viewed as a significantly greater barrier for potential than for current participants strongly suggests that this difference may be as much attributable to different inclinations toward the arts as to free time per se.

This difference in preferences is revealed most clearly by the fact that current participants are, of course, already involved in the arts and target populations are not. It is also suggested, as noted above, by the target populations' greater attraction to other leisure activities. What remains unclear, however, is whether this difference is due to prior negative arts experiences among the target groups or to a more general unfamiliarity with what the arts have to offer.

In this context, it is instructive to compare the difference between the scores for current participants and target populations on the individual items in the table. In every case, the respondents viewed these items as posing more of a barrier to target populations than to current participants. Moreover, prior experience with the arts is not a particularly important barrier to either group; nor is the difference between these groups large. By contrast, the two measures showing the largest differences between the two groups—would feel uncomfortable and not sure what the organization does—both appear to be related to the target population's uncertainty or misgivings about arts organizations and what they have to offer. Indeed, the third major difference between the two groups—the perception of elitism—reflects a similar sense of misgiving about the unfamiliar.

It is also interesting to note in this context the high importance assigned to "not enough time" versus the much lower importance assigned to "hours inconvenient." The first of these relates specifically to individuals' perception of the "busyness" of their lives and the relative attractiveness of the arts versus non-art leisure alternatives as a way to spend free time. The second refers to how an organization's schedule of activities fits with potential participants' available time. Clearly, the respondents viewed the first as a major problem, but not the second. Since Americans' free time is increasingly fragmented, these two findings are not necessarily inconsistent, but it seems likely that something more is operating here. Indeed, we believe these complaints about not having any available free time only partly stem from the pace of everyday life and the difficulty of adding the arts onto a list of other leisure activities. They also are a convenient way to describe a more general uncertainty and in some cases misgivings about the arts that stem more from a lack of information than from a host of prior negative experiences.

Somewhat less important but still cited frequently were three practical barriers—difficulties finding childcare, difficulties associated with getting to artistic venues, and the lack of information about the programs offered—and one perceptual barrier—the belief that the art form had no appeal. These were viewed as most important in their categories.

Table B.9 breaks out these data to show the distinctions across the three different types of organizations surveyed. These results generally have the same patterns found in the previous table, but there are some interesting differences. The canon-focused organizations, for example, reported that perceptual and personal circumstances are more important barriers to getting target populations involved in their activities. They also viewed costs as a more significant

Table B.9

Assessments of Barriers to Participation by the Three Types of Organizations

| | Type of Organization | | | | | |
| | Canon-Focused | | Community-Focused | | Creativity-Focused | |
Barrier	Current Partici- pants	Target Population	Current Partici- pants	Target Population	Current Partici- pants	Target Population
Perceptual						
No appeal	2.4	3.3	2.0	2.7	1.5	2.8
Hard to connect	2.1	3.0	1.9	2.4	1.5	2.1
Uncomfortable	1.8	3.4	1.8	2.7	1.7	2.8
Elitist	1.9	3.1	1.7	2.4	1.4	1.9
Personal circumstances						
Not enough time	3.2	3.8	2.9	3.1	3.2	3.3
Other leisure activities	2.6	3.7	2.6	3.3	3.1	3.4
No one to go with	1.9	2.6	1.7	2.2	1.7	2.0
Wouldn't understand interest	1.4	2.1	1.4	1.6	2.4	2.7
Practical						
Childcare problems	2.6	3.2	2.1	2.5	2.6	2.5
Inaccessibility	2.2	2.7	2.0	2.9	2.7	3.4
Not sure what organization does	1.9	3.0	2.2	3.4	1.9	3.0
Hours inconvenient	1.7	1.9	1.5	1.7	1.8	1.8
Location unsafe	1.7	2.1	1.7	2.2	1.5	1.8
Costs too much	1.9	2.9	1.8	2.2	1.5	1.8
Prior experience	1.7	2.3	1.6	2.1	1.6	2.0

NOTE: Survey asked about importance of barrier. 1 = not at all; 2 = little; 3 = fair amount; 4 = much; 5 = very much.

obstacle for target populations. Creativity-focused organizations, however, reported that access was a notably bigger problem for both current participants and target populations.

Although these differences are suggestive, it is difficult to know whether they reflect differences in the types of participants the organizations are trying to attract, differences in the activities of the organizations themselves, or perhaps a combination of both. For example, according to Table B.2 (shown earlier), canon-focused organizations place a higher priority on diversifying participation (that is, on attracting groups not currently involved with the arts) than do either creativity- or community-focused organizations. Thus, one might expect that changing target populations' attitudes might be particularly important for canon-focused organizations—a fact that might account for the greater importance they attach to perceptual barriers. On the other hand, canon-focused organizations are also more established and wealthier than the other two types of organizations, so they may also be perceived as more elite and less comfortable environments by those not inclined toward the arts. Creativity-focused organizations, in contrast, were reported as being much more focused on deepening participation. In this case, perceptual barriers, which often involve changing individuals' attitudes toward the arts may pose less of a problem.

DEVELOPING AND IMPLEMENTING TACTICS

Once an organization has identified and collected information on its target populations, including both the motivations for and obstacles to increasing participation, it then needs to consider the tactics it will use to meet its participation goals. As a first step, organizations need to consider how to publicize their programs and activities so that potential participants are aware of what they have to offer. In addition, organizations must consider what types of programs and activities to offer, where and when to schedule them, what prices (if any) to charge, and how to create an atmosphere that attracts potential participants. This section describes the various tactics used by the arts organizations we surveyed, how intensively they used them, and how effective they believed them to be.

How Organizations Publicize Their Activities

We asked the organizations about how they publicized their activities: (1) what techniques they use, (2) how often they use those techniques, and (3) whether they thought those techniques were effective. We measure effectiveness as the percentage of organizations that use a particular technique and also rate it as "very effective." Table B.10 provides the results.

It is clear from our results that the organizations we interviewed place a high priority on publicizing their activities and use a combination of techniques to do so. Seven of these ten techniques were used by close to 90 percent or more of these organizations, and no technique was used by fewer than 50 percent. All organizations frequently used word of mouth and free publicity they receive in the media, and almost all use direct mail. Five other techniques—presentations to community groups, use of community collaborators, handouts, paid media advertisements, and the Internet—were used by between 80 and 95 percent of the organizations but less often. The two least popular techniques—personal phone calls and billboards—were also used less frequently.

Although we did not ask respondents to explain the reasons for their usage patterns, at least two factors, effectiveness and availability of resources, appeared most important. The effectiveness of different techniques varies depending on their reach (who hears or reads them) and their ability to convey the

Table B.10

Use and Effectiveness of Outreach Techniques

Technique	Percentage of Organizations Using Technique	Frequency of Use[a]	Percentage of Organizations That Find Technique "Very Effective"
Word of mouth	100	4.3	41
Free media	100	4.3	31
Direct mail	98	4.4	40
Presentations to community groups	95	3.0	12
Community collaborators	92	3.5	20
Handouts	89	3.0	4
Paid media	87	3.2	29
Internet	79	4.1	18
Telephone calls	69	2.8	13
Billboards	51	1.9	6

[a]Frequency of use: 1 = not at all; 2 = little; 3 = fair amount; 4 = much; 5 = very much.

desired message. Individuals use a variety of ways to get information about their leisure choices, such as talking to friends, listening to radio, watching TV, reading, and attending community meetings. Although the ways that individuals gather this information may be similar, the specific sources they use vary depending on who their friends are, what newspapers they read, what stations they listen to, what associations they belong to, and where they live. Thus, in choosing how to advertise, arts organizations need to consider whom they are trying to reach and where and how these groups get their information.

Methods of communication also differ in their ability to convey the intended message. Messages conveyed by friends or family members and by organizations with which the individual is familiar are likely to be given more credibility than messages on billboards or in media commercials. Stories about the arts reported in the media also have greater credibility than advertisements.

The frequency of use of the various information sources may also vary across organizations depending on how much they cost (measured not only in dollars but in terms of available time and expertise) and what resources the organization has available. Use of the Internet, for example, requires more than a basic knowledge of computers and programming—something that not all arts organizations possess. Similarly, telephone calls to prospective participants require sufficient staff or volunteers to make the calls. Even the use of community resources—either community collaborators or presentations to community groups—requires staff to meet with these groups, convince them to collaborate, and then arrange for that collaboration. In sum, when considering how to spread the message about their institutions and their activities, organizations need to weigh both the effectiveness of these techniques and the resources that are required to employ them.

How, then, do the organizations we interviewed evaluate the effectiveness of the various information techniques and how does their use compare with their reported effectiveness? First, no single technique was rated as effective by more than 41 percent of the organizations that used it. The two techniques that were consistently rated most effective—direct mail and word of mouth—rely on an established link between the organization and the target population. Word of mouth relies on contacts among family and friends of potential participants, and direct mailings are sent out either to those who have already visited the organization or to those who are on a mailing list that the organization has obtained from some other organization (and thus might be expected to have attended there). Thus, information obtained from these sources may be given greater credibility than that obtained from other sources. Free publicity in the form of general interest stories about the organization published by the local press and paid advertising are also rated as effective by a substantial number of organizations. This finding may be due to the greater reach of these techniques.

Second, organizations tend to use the techniques they believe to be effective. For example, the three most effective techniques (direct mail, word of mouth, and free media) are used by more organizations and used more frequently than other techniques. Techniques used with moderate frequency are rated as effective by somewhat fewer organizations (between 10 and 29 percent). The techniques used least frequently (such as billboards) were not viewed as very effective.

There are, however, three exceptions to this pattern:

- Handouts are used by 90 percent of all organizations even though few organizations view them as effective.

- The media are used relatively infrequently despite the fact that many organizations view the media as effective, probably because of the high cost of this technique.

- Telephone solicitations are also used infrequently despite being viewed as moderately effective, probably because of the cost in both money and time required to carry them out.

Table B.11 displays our survey findings in terms of the three types of organizations. The table shows that all organizations rely very heavily on word of mouth

Table B.11

Assessments of Use and Effectiveness of Outreach Techniques by the Three Types of Organizations

| | Type of Organization | | | | | |
| | Canon-Focused | | Community-Focused | | Creativity-Focused | |
Outreach Technique	Frequency of Use[a]	Effectiveness[b]	Frequency of Use	Effectiveness	Frequency of Use	Effectiveness
Word of mouth	4.2	35	4.4	42	4.6	64
Free media	4.4	33	4.6	33	3.2	21
Direct mail	4.3	37	4.5	47	4.2	29
Presentation to community groups	2.9	8	2.9	14	3.7	21
Community collaborator	3.2	12	3.9	28	3.6	21
Handouts	2.6	4	3.5	6	3.3	0
Paid media	3.6	31	3.0	22	2.4	7
Telephone calls	2.5	14	3.3	3	2.8	7
Billboards	2.1	4	1.8	3	1.4	0

[a]Frequency of use: 1 = not at all; 2 = little; 3 = fair amount; 4 = much; 5 = very much.
[b]Effectiveness: Percentage of organizations rating the technique "very effective."

and direct mail to publicize their activities and that they avoid advertising on billboards. Their use of other techniques varies. Canon- and community-focused organizations rely quite a lot on the media to publicize their activities—especially on stories in the media but also, to a lesser degree, on purchased media advertisements. Creativity-focused organizations, in contrast, are not only less likely to have stories about their activities appear in the media, but they are also much less likely to place paid ads in the media. Instead, they rely on word of mouth and various types of direct outreach into communities, such as presentations to community groups, referrals from community collaborators, and handouts to the community. Canon-focused organizations are least inclined to use these sources. The techniques of community-focused organizations generally fall in between these two groups.

These organizations also differ in their assessment of the effectiveness of different techniques. By and large, these effectiveness ratings correlate closely with the intensity with which techniques are used. (The correlation coefficient between intensity of use and effectiveness is quite high, $r = 0.85$.) There are, however, some noteworthy differences in this respect. Although all three types of organizations view word of mouth, free media, and direct mail as effective and use them frequently, canon- and community-focused organizations also believe paid media advertisements are effective, while creativity-oriented organizations generally do not. However, creativity-focused and, to a lesser extent, community-focused organizations find community-focused techniques effective, while canon-focused organizations do not.

Other Tactics Used to Increase Participation

In addition to asking organizations how they publicize their activities, we also asked them what other tactics they use to increase participation. We subsequently grouped these individual items into five general clusters:

- **Artist involvement.** Encouraging artists to interact with participants by offering discussions before and after the performance, offering workshops, and sponsoring artist residencies.

- **Programming.** Involving the community in general planning and in designing artistic programming. Linking programming to target groups by providing artistic programs that appeal to nontraditional participants and offering ethnically diverse programming.

- **Pricing.** Offering discounts or free activities and various memberships and subscriptions options.

- **Schedule and venue.** Varying the schedule (hours and days) of programming, providing programming in more accessible locations, and providing transportation to events.

- **Other practical.** Training staff to be more responsive to the public, providing more appealing and user-friendly activities, opening the facility up to other uses, and providing services or materials in other languages.

These clusters generally correspond to different types of barriers to participation. The programming cluster addresses perceptual barriers. The pricing, scheduling and venue, and other practical tactics speak to practical barriers. Finally, by attempting to improve the quality of the participation experience, the tactics involving artists address the kinds of barriers associated with previous experience. Table B.12 shows the extent to which the organizations surveyed use these techniques, how frequently they use them, and how effective they find them.

It is clear from these results that arts organizations recognize the need to deal with each of the different potential barriers to participation. Indeed, there is considerable similarity in the tactics that arts organizations use to achieve their participation goals. All but three of these tactics are used by at least two-thirds of these organizations. And even these three exceptions—providing transportation to participants, providing materials in languages other than English, and opening facilities to other uses—may represent special cases. For example,

Table B.12

Uses and Effectiveness of Various Tactics

Technique	Percentage of Organizations Using Technique	Frequency of Use[a]	Percentage of Organizations That Find Technique "Very Effective"
Artist involvement			
Involve with participants	99	3.9	16
Lectures	97	3.7	11
Workshops	95	3.6	9
Residencies	85	3.9	13
Programming			
Involve community in planning	96	3.4	19
Nontraditional programs	97	3.8	19
Ethnic programming	97	4.1	24
Involve community in programming	82	2.5	10
Pricing			
Discounts	100	4.2	32
Subscriptions/memberships	75	3.8	16
Schedule and venue			
Vary hours	95	3.6	9
Improve access	82	3.2	17
Offer transportation	53	2.0	0
Other practical			
Train staff	99	3.1	4
User friendly	84	3.8	6
Open facility	27	3.5	12
Materials in other languages	65	2.4	9

[a]Frequency of use: 1 = not at all; 2 = a little; 3 = fair amount; 4 = much; 5 = very much.

since over 80 percent of these organizations offer programming in accessible venues, it may not be necessary (or efficient) to provide direct transportation to participants. Similarly, providing materials in other languages may not be relevant to most of these organizations if most of their current and target populations are English-speaking, and opening up their facilities may not be an option for many organizations.

Not only do these organizations use the same tactics, they tend to use them with the same intensity. Perhaps the most surprising finding in this table is the universal use of discounts to attract participants, given the fact that costs were not rated as a principal barrier to participation (see Table B.8).

One apparent explanation for this finding is found in the fact that discounts were rated the most effective single tactic. The other noteworthy finding in this comparison is the relatively high effectiveness ratings given to programming tactics. By involving the community in program planning and broadening programming to include less traditional and more diverse content, organizations are appealing to what they believe to be the main motivation of participants, both current and potential: their intrinsic interest in the arts. Apart from these two results, there appears to be considerable variation in the reported effectiveness of these tactics. Since most of the organizations have a variety of target populations, with a corresponding mixture of predisposition toward the arts as well as different personal circumstances and experiences, it would be very surprising if any particular cluster of tactics was consistently rated most effective by all organizations.

Table B.13 breaks out the data on tactics for arts organizations with different purposes. This display shows that all organizations use techniques for improving the quality of the artistic experience quite frequently. The data also show that organizations with a focus on promoting individual creativity use a greater range of tactics to attract new participants and use these tactics more frequently than other organizations:

- Creativity-focused institutions rely more heavily than other organizations on using artists in their activities, involving the community in program planning, adjusting their programming to appeal to different populations, and varying pricing and practical tactics.

- Creativity-focused organizations use discounts more intensively than other organizations do, although they are less likely to use subscriptions and membership packages.

- Creativity-focused organizations vary their schedules and the location of their activities more than other arts organizations do, a practice that addresses the problem of lack of access that they ranked as a serious obstacle to their participants.

The table also presents organizations' effectiveness ratings for each tactic. Although the ratings correlate reasonably well with the intensity of usage ($r = 0.60$), the correlation is smaller than that found in the assessment of techniques for publicity and outreach. The technique rated most effective by canon-focused organizations, ethnic programming, is rated very effective by only 25 percent of these organizations. Three different techniques are rated as very effective by over 20 percent of the community-focused organizations, with discounts rated the most effective. Finally, creativity-focused organizations rank a much higher proportion of the techniques they use as effective (eight different tactics are rated as very effective by at least 20 percent of these organizations), and the most effective technique, providing discounts, is rated very effective by almost 60 percent of these organizations.

Table B.13

Ratings of Uses and Effectiveness of Various Tactics by the Three Types of Organizations

| | Type of Organization | | | | | |
| | Canon-Focused | | Community-Focused | | Creativity-Focused | |
Outreach Technique	Frequency of Use[a]	Effectiveness[b]	Frequency of Use	Effectiveness	Frequency of Use	Effectiveness
Artists						
Involve with participants	3.7	10	3.8	14	4.9	43
Lectures	3.8	8	3.6	17	3.5	0
Workshops	3.3	10	3.8	11	4.2	21
Residencies	3.1	4	3.6	19	3.8	14
Programming						
Involve community in planning	3.2	14	3.4	25	4.2	21
Nontraditional programs	3.7	19	3.7	22	4.2	7
Ethnic programs	3.8	25	4.4	19	4.5	29
Involve community in programming	2.2	2	2.6	11	3.2	21
Pricing						
Discounts	4.0	19	4.2	42	4.6	57
Memberships/ subscriptions	4.1	12	3.8	14	1.7	7
Schedule and venue						
Vary hours	3.5	6	3.5	6	3.9	21
Improve access	2.7	12	3.3	11	4.2	29
Other practical						
Train staff	3.0	4	3.3	6	3.2	0
User-friendly	3.7	4	3.8	6	3.9	7
Open facility	3.3	6	3.9	17	3.5	0
Materials in other languages	2.1	6	2.6	8	3.0	0

[a]Frequency of use: 1 = not at all; 2 = little; 3 = fair amount; 4 = much; 5 = very much.
[b]Effectiveness: Percentage of organizations rating the technique as "very effective."

KEY CHALLENGES AND RESPONSES

Most of the questions we asked the respondents were framed as direct queries about specific aspects of their operation. Although this approach facilitated comparisons across respondents by assuring consistency in responses, it limited the respondents' opportunities to express themselves more freely on these and other subjects. To provide them with this opportunity, we included two open-ended questions:

- What are the biggest challenges your organization has faced in trying to meet its participation goals?

- What do you consider to be the three most important steps that your organization has taken to meet its participation goals?

KEY CHALLENGES

Respondents emphasized three problems as the most difficult to surmount in building participation:

- **Lack of visibility**. Many organizations viewed their lack of visibility in the community as the central challenge they faced. Sometimes this issue was raised in terms of the difficulties of reaching specific populations not familiar with their organizations or the arts in general. One literary organization, for example, referred to the difficulty of reaching people who "just don't read anymore." Indeed, some organizations that were interested in deepening the level of their participants' involvement complained that "even our subscribers don't visit our museum more than once or twice a year."

- **Increasing competition with other leisure activities**. In many ways, these organizations viewed this lack of visibility as a by-product of a second major challenge that they faced—growing competition with other leisure activities. This theme was described in terms of the increasing range of options that people have available today for entertainment and the perception that people are busier than they used to be, with both men and women increasingly in the workplace and often working irregular hours. One typical comment was made by a theater organization in Seattle: "The competitive marketplace in Seattle is a challenge—there are lots of arts and other entertainment for people to spend their disposable incomes on. It's a crowded marketplace, which increases people's awareness and interest in the arts but also creates a more savvy and demanding customer."

- **Resource shortages**. Combating these two problems poses a real resource problem for most organizations. Virtually all of the organizations we interviewed identified their greatest challenge as the difficulty of balancing competing demands against their available resources. One respondent described his organization's three biggest challenges as "First, dollars; second, dollars; and third, dollars." Some described their needs in more detail: "We need funds to computerize our box office receipts so that we can track where our money is coming from and who is buying tickets." Many organizations mentioned more general needs: to develop new programming for specific target groups, conduct research on target populations, and develop new outreach initiatives. Others mentioned the need to increase their organization's ability to respond to growth or institutional change through strategic planning, hiring and training new staff, and getting their buy-in on the organizations' participation goals, and by increasing the size of their facilities.

When citing their resource constraints, what these institutions are acknowledging is not simply the obvious fact that they do not have the resources to do all the things they want to do, but also that increasing participation takes commitment, money, hard work, and time. As the long-time director of a repertory theater company put it, "The techniques that RAND and the Wallace Funds are studying are well-known; the challenge is finding the resources to do them. A lot of people have tried a lot of things to increase participation, but the techniques that really work require a lot of work and time."

These three challenges are, of course, interrelated. Because organizations are competing with a vast leisure industry for people's scarce free time, they need to get the word out about their programs and activities. This necessarily involves increasing the visibility of their institutions in the community, and that takes resources that are in short supply.

MOST IMPORTANT ACTIONS

The most important steps institutions took to address these problems and sustain participation building are summarized below.

Improving Visibility

Respondents described two sets of actions to improve the public's awareness of their institution and its programs:

- The first step was developing the message they wanted to convey. For several organizations, the key to improving their visibility was to develop a clear message or "brand image" for their organization—something that often required them to consider their institutional purpose and mission. Sometimes this involved changing their organizational image. As one respondent put it, "We were founded and run by the same individual for 23 years. . . . Over the past two years we have worked to alter our image . . . indeed we are changing the definition of literary art and don't even use that phrase any more."

- The second step was deciding how to deliver that message. Some organizations focused on improving media relations and developing promotional materials. Other organizations simply could not afford large-scale media campaigns or found it difficult to sustain the media's attention in a very diverse entertainment market. These organizations relied on their outreach efforts with community groups to publicize their programs. Our respondents repeatedly stressed that the ties they had established with community-based organizations were one of the most important steps they had taken to inform potential participants about their organizations and activities.

Building Strategic Alliances

Many organizations developed ties with a variety of community organizations and groups, with other arts organizations, and with artists. Respondents reported that these alliances were an important conduit of information, but they also emphasized that these partnerships brought them other benefits as well, such as a greater understanding of the people in the communities they were pursuing and a relationship of trust with those communities. Sometimes other organizations were able to offer the use of their facilities or other materials.

Respondents also mentioned a number of lessons they had learned about the process of building good partnerships:

- **Choosing an organization with a complementary mission.** Collaborating organizations should have complementary missions. Without common goals, organizations may never build the deep connection needed to foster mutual commitment. The alliance between Poet's House and the New York City Public Library, for example, is based on a shared commitment to fostering the appreciation of literature and recognition of each institution's distinct strengths and mutual needs.

- **Choosing organizations with complementary assets and strengths.** It is important to find organizations that can contribute skills, connections, and material assets that are complementary. Hancher Auditorium in Iowa City, for example, brought together the Colorado String Quartet with three local public libraries and three churches to perform chamber music in their spaces. This collaboration allowed musicians to perform in locations that were accessible and comfortable for their audiences. As a result, many community residents who had never before experienced chamber music bought tickets to the concert.

- **Building trust.** Relationships must be perceived as mutually beneficial. Unless arts institutions make the effort to build trust in the relationship, they run the risk of being seen as "missionaries" or "users" by collaborating organizations. It is important for institutions to identify the right people to cultivate this relationship, both on their own staff and within the collaborating organization. As the director of Poet's House explained, "The difficulty in working with organizations different from your own is getting to know each other and developing an understanding of the way the other organization works. You need to hook up with the right person to get you through the maze, someone who can translate between the two organizations."

- **Understanding mutual capabilities.** When Hancher Auditorium decided to start performing in nontraditional venues, they sought out a factory setting. This early venture was fraught with operational problems because the factory staff had no background in setting up the performance space, promoting the event within the factory, and assuming other roles necessary to mounting a production. What the staff of Hancher Auditorium learned from this experience was the importance of providing more hands-on training when collaborating with non-arts organizations in the community.

- **Maintaining commitment over the long term.** Organizations change over time—missions alter, people come and go, budgets shrink and grow. Good relationships with outside organizations can quickly deteriorate if key people depart or financial support disappears. Many of the exemplary arts organizations mentioned the fact that short-term funding undermines ongoing collaborations. They suggest a steady investment of staff time in building relationships that can weather such uncertainties in financial support.

Changes in Programming

By far the most frequently given response to the question about actions taken to increase participation was changes in program offerings. This finding is, no doubt, related to the fact that these organizations believe, as we noted earlier, that the single most important motivation for participation is the participant's interest in the arts. Thus, a wide variety of programming-related tactics were mentioned—initiation of specific programs (such as arts festivals, poetry readings, and other events) and more general strategies (such as developing programming to appeal to specific target populations and/or increasing the amount or quality of programming or both). Although these programming changes were often focused on attracting specific target groups, several organizations stressed that the key to sustained participation was "high-quality productions." As one respondent put it, "The only way to keep people coming back is to do high-quality work."

However, the respondents emphasized that it is not enough simply to develop programs likely to appeal to target populations; it is also important to anticipate the kinds of obstacles that prevent individuals from participating and to take steps to overcome those barriers. One way of doing this is to project a different institutional image. As one respondent put it, their institution developed new programming to project a vibrant image: "We wanted our programming to stand for something—diversity, freshness, extreme, smart, savvy, and producer of American voices." Other respondents stressed their work to make audiences familiar and more comfortable with their programs, particularly the more demanding programs, by developing activities such as lectures and workshops before and after performances. They also mentioned their efforts to schedule their events so as to minimize problems of access, convenience, and cost.

Improving Operations

Although the majority of these organizations focused on the tactics they instituted to further their specific participation goals, quite a few of them mentioned actions that they took to improve their general organizational structure and operations.[3] In most cases, the actions mentioned directly supported participation-building activities, but they often also helped to improve the general operation of the institution.

Among the actions respondents mentioned were improved strategic planning, selecting participation goals, allocating resources according to their strategic plans, and ensuring staff commitment to the organization's participation goals and plans. They also included such structural steps as funding new positions, restructuring departments, diversifying staff, and bringing in new administrative or board leadership. Operational improvements included changes in box office practices, ticketing, record-keeping, and office management.

Some of the important steps respondents mentioned had a direct effect on the ability of the organization to pursue its more general missions. Most frequently mentioned in this context were successful initiatives to increase financial resources, such as applying for and receiving new grants and building internal resources by hiring new staff and changing board membership.

Also in this category, many respondents emphasized that their most important step in building participation was expanding or improving their facilities. Several smaller and growing organizations noted, for example, that they had moved to new quarters or substantially upgraded their existing facilities by adding more meeting or performance space, upgrading capacity, or providing eating facilities. Such capital expansion allowed them to attract and serve new participants as well as to improve the quality and range of their programming.

---

[3]It should be noted that some of these operational improvements were required as a condition of the grant from the Funds.

Overall, we found that most respondents focused their observations on the specific tactics that they used—with a particular emphasis on the steps they took to attract participants and marshal the resources they needed. However, they also commented on the need to pay heed to the other elements of an integrative approach to the participation process by talking about the importance of strategic planning in choosing their participation goals and measuring and evaluating their progress. Indeed, we were struck by the fact that when viewed in the aggregate, the respondents mentioned elements from each of the different steps that identify an integrative approach to building participation.

SITE VISITS TO FUNDS GRANTEES SELECTED FOR IN-DEPTH INTERVIEWS

Organization	City	Artistic Discipline	Region	City Type
Ballet Arizona	Phoenix	Dance	W	Small city/ suburban
California Institute of the Arts	Los Angeles	Visual arts	W	Urban
Cleveland Museum of Art	Cleveland	Visual arts	MW	Urban
Cornerstone Theater	Los Angeles	Theater	W	Urban
Freedom Theatre	Philadelphia	Theater	NE	Urban
Hancher Auditorium	Iowa City	Presenter (performing arts)	MW	Urban
Old Town School of Folk Music	Chicago	Folk arts (music)	MW	Urban
Poet's House	New York	Literary arts	NE	Urban
St. Louis Symphony Orchestra	St. Louis	Music	S	Small city/ suburban
The Loft	Minneapolis	Literary arts	MW	Urban
University Musical Society	Ann Arbor	Presenter (music)	MW	Small city/ suburban
Walker Arts Center	Minneapolis	Visual arts	MW	Small city/ suburban
Western Folklife Center	Elko	Folk arts (multidisciplinary)	W	Rural

Aday, LuAnn, and Stephen M. Shortell. "Indicators and Predictors of Health Services Utilization," in Stephen J. Williams and Paul R. Torrens (eds.), *Introduction to Health Services*, Wiley Medical, John Wiley and Sons, 1998.

American Assembly. "The Arts and the Public Purpose," in Gigi Bradford, Michael Gary, and Glenn Wallach (eds.), *The Politics of Culture*, New York: The New Press, 2000, pp. 64–70.

Americans for the Arts. *Highlights from a Nationwide Survey of the Attitudes of the American People Towards the Arts*, Vol. 7, prepared for the American Council for the Arts, the National Assembly of Local Arts Agencies, conducted by Louis Harris, 1996.

AMS Planning and Research. *A Practical Guide To Arts Participation Research*, Report #30, Washington, D.C.: NEA, 1995.

Bart, C. K. "Product Strategy and Formal Structure," *Strategic Management Journal*, Vol. 7, 1986, pp. 283–311.

Baumol, William J., and William Bowen. *Performing Arts: The Economic Dilemma*, New York: Twentieth Century Fund, 1966.

Bergonzi, Louis, and Julia Smith. *Effects of Arts Education on Participation in the Arts*, Washington, D.C.: NEA, 1996.

Butsch, Richard. *The Making of American Audiences: From Stage to Television, 1750–1990*, Cambridge: Cambridge University Press, 2000.

Chapman, Laura. "Arts Education as a Political Issue: The Federal Legacy," in Ralph A. Smith and Ronald Berman (eds.), *Public Policy and the Aesthetic Interest: Critical Essays on Defining Cultural and Educational Relations*, Urbana, IL: University of Illinois Press, 1992, pp. 119–136.

Cherbo, Joni M., and Margaret J. Wyszomirski. "Mapping the Public Life of the Arts in America," in *The Public Life of the Arts in America*, New Brunswick, NJ: Rutgers University Press, 2000.

Cobb, Nina K. *Looking Ahead: Private Sector Giving to the Arts and the Humanities*, Washington, D.C.: President's Committee on the Arts and the Humanities, 1996.

Cyert, R. M., and J. G. March. *A Behavioral Model of the Firm*, Englewood Cliffs, NJ: Prentice Hall, March 1963.

Deveaux, Scott. *Jazz in America: Who's Listening?* Washington, D.C.: NEA, 1994.

DiMaggio, Paul J. "Decentralization of Arts Funding from the Federal Government to the States," in Stephen Benedict (ed.), *Public Money and the Muse: Essays on Government Funding for the Arts*, New York: W.W. Norton Company, 1991.

DiMaggio, Paul. "Nonprofit Organizations in the Production and Distribution of Culture," in W. Powell (ed.), *The Nonprofit Sector: A Research Handbook*, New Haven, CT: Yale University Press, 1987.

DiMaggio, Paul, et al. *Audience Studies of the Performing Arts and Museums: A Critical Review*, Report #9, Washington, D.C.: NEA, 1978.

Felton, Marianne V. "On the Assumed Inelasticity of Demand for the Performing Arts," *Journal of Cultural Economics*, Vol. 16, No. 1, June 1992.

Ford Foundation. *The Finances of the Performing Arts*, Vol. 2, New York: The Ford Foundation, 1974.

Gray, Charles M. *Turning On and Tuning In: Media Participation in the Arts*, Washington, D.C.: NEA, 1995.

Heilbrun, James, and Charles Gray. *The Economics of Art and Culture*, Cambridge: Cambridge University Press, 1993.

Heinz Endowments. *Bringing the Arts to Life, Arts and Culture Program*, Pittsburgh, PA: The Heinz Endowments, 1999.

Holak, Susan L., et al. "Analyzing Opera Attendance: The Relative Impact of Managerial and Environmental Variables," *Empirical Studies of the Arts*, Vol. 4, No. 2, 1986.

Keagen, Carol. *Public Participation in Classical Ballet: A Special Analysis of the Ballet Data Collected in the 1982 and 1985 Surveys of Public Participation in the Arts*, Washington, D.C.: NEA, 1987.

Kelley, John R. *Freedom to Be: A New Sociology of Leisure*, New York: Macmillan, 1987.

Kelley, John R., and Valeria J. Freisinger. *21st Century Leisure: Critical Issues*, Boston, MA: Allyn and Bacon, 2000.

Lemmons, Jack R. *American Dance 1992: Who's Watching? Who's Dancing?* Washington, D.C.: NEA, 1996.

Love, Jeffrey. *Patterns of Multiple Participation in the Arts: An Analysis of 1982, 1985, and 1992 SPPA Data*, Washington, D.C.: NEA, 1995.

McCarthy, Kevin F., and Laura Zakaras. *Guide to the Literature on Participation in the Arts*, Santa Monica, CA: RAND, forthcoming.

Morrison, Bradley G., and Julie Gordon Dalgleish. *Waiting in the Wings: A Larger Audience for the Arts and How to Develop It*, New York: Allworth Press, 1987.

Nardone, J. M. "Is the Movie Industry Countercyclical?" *Cycles*, Vol. 33, No. 3, April 1982.

National Endowment for the Arts. *1997 Survey of Public Participation in the Arts*. NEA Research Division Report 39. National Endowment for the Arts, 1998.

Orend, Richard J., and Carol Keegan. *Education and Arts Participation: A Study of Arts Socialization and Current Arts-Related Activities Using 1982 and 1992 SPPA Data*, Washington, D.C.: NEA, 1996.

Peters, Monica, and Joni Maya Cherbo. *Americans' Personal Participation in the Arts: 1992: A Monograph Describing Data from the Survey of Public Participation in the Arts*, Washington, D.C.: NEA, 1996.

Putnam, Robert. *Bowling Alone: The Collapse and Revival of American Community*, New York: Simon and Schuster, 2000.

Renz, Loren, and Steven Lawrence. *Arts Funding: An Update on Foundation Trends*, third ed., New York: The Foundation Center, 1998.

Robinson, John P. *Arts Participation in America: 1982–1992*, Washington, D.C.: NEA, 1993.

Robinson, John P., et al. *Public Participation in the Arts: Final Report on the 1982 Survey*, Washington, D.C.: NEA, 1985.

Robinson, John P., and Geoffrey Godbey. *Time for Life: The Surprising Ways Americans Use Their Time*, second ed., Pennsylvania: Penn State University Press, 1997.

Schor, Juliet B. *The Overworked American: The Unexpected Decline of Leisure*, New York: Basic Books, 1991.

Schuster, Mark D. *The Audience for American Art Museums*, Washington, D.C.: NEA, 1991.

Shortell, S., and A. Kaluzny. "Organizational Theory and Health Services Management," in Stephen M. Shortell and Arnold D. Kaluzny (eds.), *Health Care Management: Organization Design and Behavior,* third ed., Albany, NY: Delmar Publishers, 1994.

Stebbins, Robert. *Amateurs, Professionals, and Serious Leisure,* Montreal: McGill-Queens University Press, 1992.

Stigler, George J., and Gary S. Becker. "De Gustibus Non Est Disputandum," *American Economic Review,* Vol. 67, No. 2, 1977, pp. 76–90.

Throsby, C. David, and Glenn Winter. *The Economics of the Performing Arts,* New York: St. Martin's Press, 1979.

Toffler, Alvin. *The Culture Consumers: A Study of Art and Affluence in America.* New York: St. Martin's Press, 1964.

Urice, John K. "The Future of the State Arts Agency Movement in the 1990's: Decline and Effect," *Journal of Arts Management, Law (and Society),* Vol. 22, No. 1, Spring 1992, pp. 19–32.

Useem, Michael. "Corporate Support for Culture and the Arts," in Margaret J. Wyszomirski and Pat Clubb (eds.), *The Cost of Culture: Patterns and Prospects of Private Arts Patronage.* New York: ACA Books, 1990.

Vogel, Harold. *Entertainment Industry Economics: A Guide for Financial Analysis,* Cambridge, U.K.: Cambridge University Press, 2000.

Walker, Chris, et al. *Reggae to Rachmaninoff: How and Why People Participate in Arts and Culture,* Washington, D.C.: Urban Institute, 2000.

Zaltman, Gerald, et al., *Understanding Peoples' Thoughts and Feelings About the Arts,* prepared for The Howard Heinz Endowment, Pittsburgh, PA, 1998.